AF480823

Financial Markets
Adaptation and the journey beyond

Pramod Kesav N

NOTION PRESS

NOTION PRESS
India. Singapore. Malaysia.

Disclaimer

Foreword

This book, Financial Markets: Adaptation and the journey beyond, gives a perspective on the different Indian Financial and Global Financial Management topics adapting the different Financial Derivatives as tools and instruments in a journal depicting Investment decisions, Portfolio Management and Financial Corporate fundamentals as it is evident in usual Mentoring and Coaching sessions where a Financial Apprentice records learning notes in a Financial Expedition Specialist's journals and backlogs.

Basic and fundamental learning is attempted on all these topics that the student or learner goes through in a Business Administration course specializing in Finance.

Hope it is easily readable and gives a chance or helps a novice to attain expert levels faster.

Happy Reading!

Pramod Kesav N
Payikkattu, Kalavamkodam, Cherthala, Alappuzha,
Kerala, India

Contents

Indian Financial System

1

An Introduction to the Indian Financial System

What is a Financial System?

The term financial system conveys that it is a set of related services or activities where it all comes together to achieve certain common goals or common purpose. Whether it is mobilization of savings or the efficient, equitable, and effective allocation of investments, Finance acts as a bridge between the present needs and future needs of the society. It goes without a question that the actual need in India is an efficient Indian Financial System so that all benefits of voluntary and market-based decision making can be obtained which may lead to economic transformation on the basis of institutional and functional jurisprudence.

Influencing savings, growth and investment capital formation, Indian Financial system includes different markets, institutions, instruments, services, and its different mechanisms of financial sectors.

Definition of Financial System

Robinson has defined the primary function of Financial System as a link between investments and savings so that it permits Portfolio adjustments in the composition of existing wealth and provides a link between investment and savings for the creation of new wealth.

From Robinson's definition, the primary function of Financial System is in the mobilization of savings and their distribution for investments in the industry thereby simulating economic growth by accelerating capital formation.

The process of accelerating capital formation depends upon savings, finance (offering loans) and investments in financial instruments and services, financial institutions, and markets. It also goes without a question the importance of supervisory control and regulations when one introspects Financial System, in particular the Indian Financial System. Thus, it can be said that Financial Management is an integral part of any Financial System.

According to a Hypothesis by Goldsmith, there exists empirical evidence for separation of savings and investments in a functional form, of creation of Financial Institutions, and its mechanisms of Financial Instruments as well as enlargement of financial assets increasing efficiency of investments raising ratio of capital formation so that two channels are formed in form, National Production and Financial activities increasing the Rate of Growth.

This rate of growth is impeccable in diversified segments of the economy and their inter-relationships can be illustrated as given.

In a modern economy, a financial system provides essential services. The use of widely accepted medium of Exchange which is stable reduces the cost of transactions. It no matter facilitates trade which improves specialization in Production. Savings in Financial Form is encouraged by Financial Assets with attractive yield, risk characteristics, and liquidity. Financial Intermediaries increase the efficiency of Resource usage whenever they evaluate alternate investments by monitoring the activities of borrowers. An economic agent may price, pool and exchange Risks in the market and it is enabled in most cases by an access to a variety of financial instruments.

Trading an efficient use of resources is one of the way savings and risk taking becomes corner-stones of a growing economy.   With the help of an active supporting Financial System, a country could make this feasible and hence Financial System is identified as the most catalysing agent for economic growth and acts as one of the key inputs of development.

Classifications
(Indian Financial System)

Indian Financial System is classified as, Organized Sector and Unorganized Sector.

Before discussing that, we should also be aware of another classification of Financial Services, which is divided into Users of Financial Services as well as Providers of Financial Services. Financial Institutions are Users of Financial services because they sell services to Households, Business, and the government. Commercial Banks, Merchant Banks, Insurance Companies and Investment Trusts and Mutual Funds may be some of the providers of Financial Services.

Now we come back and discuss Organized Sector and Unorganized Sector in the Indian Financial System.

Organized Indian Financial System

A Range of Financial Instruments along with a well-developed Money Market and Capital Market, alongside an impressive network of bank make the Organized Indian Financial System. Cooperative and Commercial Banks provide Short Term funds. Nine-tenth of such banking business is controlled by less than twenty-eight leading banks, many of whom, have gone through Mergers or Consolidations. In addition to Commercial banks that exist in the country, there is in existence, a network of land development banks and co-operative banks at state, district, and block level.

In the organized Indian Financial System, it is estimated that there are around two third share of the total assets in the entire Indian Financial system. Many Indian banks in the Organized Indian Financial System, have diversified into areas such as Leasing, Factoring, Merchant Banking and Mutual Funds.

In short, the Organized Indian Banking System comprises of,

- Cooperative Banks,
- Development Banking system in Public Sector,
- Development Banking system in Private Sector,
- Money Markets and
- Financial Companies or Financial Institutions.

Recently, the Indian Financial System has developed into three areas, being, Cooperative, State, and Private. The Rural and Urban areas are serviced by Cooperative Sector alongside Cooperative bodies with a National Status.

Unorganized Indian Financial System

The unorganized Indian Financial System comprises of Money Lenders, lending Pawn-brokers, Traders, Landlords, Indigenous Bankers, etc. Even though RBI (Reserve Bank of India) does not control the unorganized Indian Financial System which may comprise of a host of chit funds, financial companies, and investment companies, but all are governed by rules and regulations and are therefore under the gambit of the Monetary authorities in India.

Indian Banking System

Increased banking services is a must due to the spread of banking habitat and the development of the economy.

Normally in India, the structure of the Banking System is determined by Economic Factors and Legal Factors.

Banking Regulations by their very nature can be categorized into two types namely, Regulations that result in new Banks and the next, which is by way of Legislation affecting a Bank's structure more due to Mergers, Nationalization, and Liquidation.

Government regulations are a direct result of National objectives and aspirations and it no doubt has a lasting influence on the Banking structure.

Reserve Bank of India

RBI is the central bank of the country and heads all banks in this group of Commercial Banks, which may be further divided into Scheduled and Non-Scheduled Banks.

Commercial Banking system happens in both Private Sector and Public Sector. Some of the Private Sector banks are new banks that have sprung up recently, cooperative banks included in the second schedule, foreign banks in India, and other non-scheduled banks. Some of the Public Sector banks are SBI, Nationalized Banks, Regional Rural Banks, etc.

Cooperative Sector Banks

In order to replace the village moneylender, cooperative banking sector has been developed in the country, where one should know that the village moneylender, remain the only source of rural finance; until cooperative sectors banks were developed, as the terms in which the village moneylender made money lending was damaging and at exorbitant rates.

Although this sector banks receive concessional finance from the Reserve Bank of India, the rules and regulations exist and the governance of this sector is by the state legislation. From the perspective of Money Market, Cooperative Sector Banks are said to lie between Organized Markets and Unorganized Market (Financial System).

Primary Cooperative Credit Societies

An association of Borrowers and Non-Borrowers is what makes the Primary Cooperative Credit Societies. Society's funds are from deposits of members, from Share Capital as well as from Central Cooperative banks. The borrowing powers of the Primary Cooperative societies and of the members are at a fixed rate. The loans given to the members are used by the members for the purchase of fertilizers, pesticides, and made use of in the purchase of cattle and fodder.

Central Cooperative Banks

Central Cooperative Banks are federations of primary credit societies in a district and they conduct the business of a joint stock bank.

State Cooperative Banks

State Cooperative Banks are a federation of Central Cooperative Banks and lend money to central cooperative banks and societies but do not lend money directly to the farmers. It acts as a watch dog of the cooperative banking structure in the State. The funds for distribution as loans are obtained from Share Capital, Deposits, Loans and Overdrafts from the Reserve Bank of India.

Land Development Banks

Land Development Banks meet the long-term credit requirements of the farmers for development purposes. It is organized in three levels, namely, State, Central, and Primary Levels. It provides credit to farmers for purchase of equipment like pump sets, tractors, machineries, fencing purposes, reclamation of land, well digging, etc. Land Development Banks are cooperative institutions and they lend money as loans based on the security of farmer's immovable properties.

Money Market

Money Market is to do with the supply and demand of funds that can be invested. It is the sum-total of all the short-term funds available in the market. It provides a mechanism whereby short-term funds are borrowed or let out.

Capital Market

Capital Market is where long term and medium-term financial needs of the business are met by the financial institutions. These institutions in turn are classified as development banks and investing institutions on the basis of financial mechanisms adopted and the nature of their activities.

Investing institutions are made up of those financial institutions who collects the savings of people and offer people their own shares and stocks which provide the much-needed long term funds by corporations, especially in the form of direct investments in securities, or by way of business enterprises' underwriting of capital issues.

2

Public Debt

Public Debt is raised by the Government to cover for the differences between budgeted receipts (government income) and budgeted payments (expenses). There are pressing significance when one thinks about Public Debt, the consequences mainly on the Production activities and the Distribution activities of a country. Thus, Public Debt is Government Debt or State Debt.

The State generally borrows Public Debt to,

- Meet Budget deficits,
- Finance Developmental activities and
- To cover other expenses of the Government.

Classifications of Public Debt

Public Debt can be classified as External Debt and Internal Debt.

External Debts are cumulative amounts raised outside of the Country by the Government and Governmental bodies whereas Internal Debts are loans raised within the country.

Internal Debt

Let us see what is Internal Debt portion of the Public Debt.

Internal Debt of the Indian Government comprises of special securities issued to the Reserve Bank and

Financial Institutions, market loans, treasury bills, and other Liabilities. Other Liabilities which are rupee debt under the Public Account comprises of Small Savings, State Provident Funds, Public Provident Funds, accounts such as Postal Insurance, Life Annuity Funds, Reserve Funds, and Special deposits.

The Indian Debt Market includes Money Market and Bond Market. Whereas in Money Market in India, the money that makes up the market is well developed with a fairly large turnover and with a wide range of financial instruments, the story with the secondary bond market is unlike the money market, is stunted and very primitive.

Hence, we can list down the Instruments traded in the Debt Market as, Securities from the Government of India, Treasury Bills, Government Guaranteed Bonds, State Government Securities, PSU Bonds, Commercial papers, Certificates of Deposits, and Corporate Debentures.

There also exists aspirants of the Debt Market, which are fund managers, brokers, and merchant bankers who also plan to evolve into Self-Regulatory Organizations in the long run. However, the Principal Regulatory authorities of the Debt Market are the Government of India, the Reserve Bank of India, the Department of Company Affairs, the Ministry of Finance, and the Securities and Exchange Board of India.

External Debt

As per the Constitution of India, Central Government and not the State Government has access to External Debt.

However, the Central Government has so far not been borrowing on a commercial platform and all its borrowings are limited to assistance from external sources, which are mainly, multilateral sources like the IBRD (International Bank for Reconstruction and Development), IDA (International Development Association) and other Governments of friendly countries.

In addition to this, Public Enterprise in India is allowed to resort to external borrowings provided it is on concessional terms through lending arrangements made by the Government of India, though there is a recent move to dispense with the Intermediation of Government in the case of Public Enterprise borrowing.

In India, the external debt at present is made based on the original maturity. The measure of Long-term sustainability of debt and overall solvency of a country is reflected in conventional analysis by keeping track of the Stock of Debt by original maturity expressed as a ratio of GDP. However, the recent developments of Crises in Asia have shown that in an otherwise solvent economy, whenever debt by original maturity is reflected, suffers a serious liquidity problem, when the burden of servicing the debt exceeds foreign exchange reserve, seriously undermining a country's ability to contract new debt or extend the existing old debt.

Upon a shift in market sentiments, what gets reflected again is a debt crisis for the country, which may not be on the radar to issue a warning signal in the standard measures of Sustainability of Debt.

In the context of Short-Term Debt, this observation is especially true, and true is the fact that there is an inability experienced to capture cross-border bank liabilities and roll-overs imposing a downward trend or bias on debt, measured in terms of maturity that is original. But the Debt by Residual maturity, in the Foreign Exchange Market, presents a true picture in terms of its impact on Maturing Debt and enables the Authorities to fine-tune the Debt Management Instruments, prospectively, which may include, interest rates and ceilings ensuring sustainable external payments that bring about the integration of external debt statistics with Balance of Payments. The irony faced by the country may be a higher external payment, despite the existence of a declining short-term debt to foreign currency assets.

Despite the increasing trend of External Debt in early 2000, the key indicators have considerably improved over time.

In the later parts of the first decade of the 21st century, short-term debt to foreign currency assets has also declined consistently by a decimal point confirming that within the Public Debt, 10% makes up total external debt, and 90 percent makes up total Internal Debt. A unique feature of External Debt is its structure, which is why, multilateral financial institutions like the IMF are not worried, since 34% of our external debt is owed to the IMF or World bank when only 18% is owed to bilateral aid agencies. This in addition to the fact that over a third of our External debt is concessional debt gives us relief in matters of discussing External Debt in comparison to similar but other countries.

Debt Ownership

Based on a survey conducted by the Reserve Bank of India, on the Ownership pattern of Government securities, reveals that more than 90% of government securities lie with the Government and its quasi-institutions as opposed to 10% which lie with the individuals. Also, the following assumption does not hold true, the assumption being, an increase in the interest rate on treasury bills and government securities will attract large amounts of savings from the household sector.

This is called the Internal Debt trap and there exist four parameters to counter any or all such arguments about the rise in interest rates helping or attracting large amounts of savings from the household sector. Firstly, it is generally argued that government borrowing facilitates asset creation which in turn takes care of debt payment. This assumption is not true because in most cases, governmental borrowings are in most cases used for non-developmental expenditure, especially non-plan-based activities. Secondly, it is assumed that out of public borrowings, a significant portion is invested in enterprises that are productive. However, the real fact of the matter is that there are significant delays in the fruitification of any assets made out of government borrowing and as a result, the growth rate in debt burden continues to be unabated in addition to the interest burden that gets piled up, after every passing year. Thirdly, as we know Government Securities and Treasury bills have a captive market where the share of the household sector in that captive market is abysmally small. As we know, the situation is not going to change in the next few years. Lastly, with the acceptance of monetary measures targeted by the government, the RBI can't absorb the government's loan tranches in particular the residuary portion of government loans as it was done some years ago.

So, the Internal Debt Trap exists as is so convincingly supported by the counterarguments. Next, we will take a look at the Maturity Pattern of the Debt.

Maturity Pattern

There are three classes of loans offered by the Central Government and State Government, maturity wise it is, Short-Term, Medium-Term, and Long-Term Loans.

Short-Term loans are for a period of 1-5 years whereas Medium-Term loans are for a period of 5 to 10 years and long-term loans are for a period beyond 10 years. Of the Central Government Debt, about 17% are short-term, 22% are medium-term and 61% is long-term in nature. The Government reserves long-term loans for capital outlay projects so it gives sufficient time for developmental outlays, where the maturities are well distributed. Also, one has to keep in mind that there are no double-dated loans, none are repaid before the maturity date.

Secondary Debt Market

The system of Primary dealers would enable the development of an orderly secondary market. The M-T-M (Move to Market) related rates of interest strengthens the development of the secondary market, with primary and secondary markets giving effective signals to each other.

Primary dealers act as market makers by giving two-way quotes for the securities. They are not the ultimate investors but they should have the capacity to hold the securities till they are able to access them in the secondary market.

Primary dealers are approved by the Reserve Bank of India and they help in placing the government securities by committed participation in auctions in Primary issues.

For Open Market Operations (OMO which is the purchase and sale of securities in the open market by central or federal banking institutions which is used to regulate the supply of money) by the Reserve Bank, the primary dealers act as a conduit for those operations and provide signals for market intervention according to the rules and guidelines given out by the Reserve Bank of India.

The RBI Guidelines for the enlistment of Primary dealers in Government Securities, relate themselves to committing to bid a minimum amount, underwrite a particular part, achieve turnover, and maintain minimum capital standards including assets such as risk-weighted assets under RBI Regulations. The Bank will on their behalf, extend Current Account and Subsidiary Ledger account facility and liquidity to support bidding commitments and give freedom to deal in money market instruments favouring OMO by RBI.

Upon successful completion, Primary Dealers are paid commission including for underwriting of the securities.

A greater amount of transparency is imparted with the development of the debt segment in the National Stock Exchange, whereby duplication of transactions is recorded by the Reserve Bank under the SGL Account. Several measures would reduce settlement risk in transactions and prevent diversification of funds in the case of transactions through SGL, including, whatever is done in the System of Delivery versus Payment (DVP) in government securities (Mumbai) to synchronize the transfer of securities with cash payment.

All the more, the liquidity of securities would improve by the existing set up of Discount and Finance House of India (DFHI) along with the setting up of Securities Trading Corporation of India (STCI) which would make attractive, holding of the Government Securities in the long run.

REPO and Reverse REPO

REPO is a repurchase agreement that is a short-term loan, where both the seller and the buyer agree to the sale and future repurchase of assets within a specific time period that is mentioned in the repurchase agreement. The seller sells the asset also may have collateral and promises to buy back the asset at a price that includes its interest at a specified time period. REPO are short-term contracts mostly overnight transactions. For example, the Central bank can boost money by buying Treasury bonds or other government debt instruments from commercial banks which infuses the commercial bank with cash and increases it reserve in the short run. Upon completion of the contract, the Central bank resells them back to the Commercial bank.

However, a reverse repo is an act of selling securities and purchase of it at a profit at a later date. For example, a bank may borrow money from the Reserve Bank at Repo Rate and lend money back to RBI at the reverse repo rate. So, this completes a session on Public Debt.

3

Merchant Banking

Introduction to Merchant Banking

The entire range of Financial Services from extending finance for investment in projects to organizing finance, and further assistance in Financial Management, acceptance of Housing business, raising issues of foreign currency bonds, raising Eurodollar loans, financing the export of capital goods, financing local authorities, etc comes under the purview of Merchant Banking. However, after SEBI abolished all categories of Merchant Banking other than Category I are mandated to manage public issues as lead managers. To recollect, Public Issues are issues of convertible securities or shares in the primary market by promoters of the Company to attract new investors where they pay the share application money.

How complex is Issue Management activity?

Issue management activity has a huge stake in the market's integrity because it affects investors' interest and as such transparency should be ensured. On a separate note, compliance is also enforced and monitored throughout this process.

To know about the first move to start Merchant Banking services, there was the placement of Banking Commission in 1972 which reported their findings on Merchant Banking Services. The Banking Commission

Report in the year 1972, favoured the setting up of a new Institution for Merchant banking that is different from Term Lending Institutions and Commercial Banks where they offer investment management and advisory services for small and medium customers who themselves are business people. The Commission then also suggested that Merchant Banking Institutions should also manage pension funds, trusts, and provident funds in India, by ensuring transparency and upholding investor interests.

Merchant Banking in India

Grindlays Bank in the year 1967 was authorized to carry on Merchant Banking Services in India and obtained a license from the Reserve Bank of India in the same year. Grindlays Bank recognized the need for an emerging entrepreneurial class for financial services that were diverse and distinct from system design and market research to production planning. They started with the management of capital assets and went on addressing the needs of Small- Scale units by providing services and management consultancy to large and medium-sized companies.

Citibank followed suit and set up its first merchant banking division in the year 1970. This division took up the task of evaluating new projects and also the tasks of assisting new entrepreneurs by raising funds through equity issues and borrowing activities. Merchant bankers by then were allowed to act as primary dealers in Government securities and as there was widespread acceptance of Management Consultancy services in the country, it also provided management consultancy services to numerous business establishments. Following the Recommendations of the Banking Commission in

1972, a lot more Indian banks started offering Merchant Banking Services notably, the Indian Bank and the State Bank of India, where the SBI's objective was to render assistance and corporate advice to medium and small entrepreneurial class.

Merchant Banking Regulations

Organized as Body Corporates, Merchant Banking Institutions were governed by the Merchant Banker's Rules issued by the Ministry of Finance and by Merchant Banker's Regulations issued by SEBI.

Now, who is a Merchant Banker, and what are the regulations that we just spoke of?

A Merchant Banker is any person who is engaged in issue management business either by making arrangements in buying, subscribing, or selling of securities as Manager, Consultant, or Advisor, and also renders Corporate Advisory in relation to such issue management efforts.

Investor's confidence depended a great deal on the efficiency of issue management functions including drafting and issuing of the Letter of Offer and Prospectus and after submitting it to SEBI for the Primary Markets, a lot of efficient work happened for the timely dispatch of refund orders and share certificates.

Merchant Banker's Regulations

Regulating the raising of funds in the primary market, the Merchant Bankers' Regulations assure the issuer of a market where they can raise resources effectively and ensures a higher degree of protection in terms of interest of the investors and merchant bankers alike. For the Merchant Banker, the Regulations provide a competitive and dynamic market with a higher standard of solvency, honesty, integrity, and competency. The regulations also mandate that anybody proposing to engage in merchant banking needs authorization from SEBI for engagements therein.

Registration and Prospectus Filing

On 5th September 1997, SEBI abolished all the categories of Merchant Bankers that are below Category 1. All Merchant Bankers operating in categories below Category 1 should now work under Category 1 status.

Merchant Bankers under Category 1 can carry on forward activities relating to Issue Management, including the preparation of Prospectus, Determination of the Financial Structure of a Company, Final Allotment of securities, refund of subscribers as well as tie up of financiers, etc.

The matters to be considered by SEBI (Securities and Exchange Bureau of India) for grant of Certificate of Registration to a Merchant Banker are,

- o Merchant Bankers must have the necessary infrastructure in place to carry forward the business of Merchant Banking,
- o Merchant Banker should be a body corporate other than a nonbanking financial company,
- o Merchant Bankers should fulfil capital adequacy of a minimum net worth of Rs. 5 crores,
- o Merchant Bankers must have employed at least 2 persons with experience to carry forward the Merchant Banking Business,
- o Merchant Banker should not be involved in litigation with the Securities Market,

- o Merchant Banker should recognize professional qualifications in Finance, Law, or Business Management and
- o Their Registration should be in the interest of the investors.

As per the advice of the Registrar of Companies, only Merchant Bankers can file a prospectus for Public Issue and should be authorized by SEBI under a given code number. Also, the Registrar of Companies is required that he or she will not register a prospectus if it is known that it has contents in the Prospectus that breach the provisions of a law or statutory rules and regulations.

Functions of Merchant Bankers

Some of the functions of Merchant Bankers are

- o Capital Restructuring,
- o Issue Management and Underwriting,
- o Portfolio Management,
- o Working Capital Finance,
- o Mergers, Amalgamations, and Takeovers and
- o Venture Capital and Lease Financing.

Capital Restructuring

This aims to reduce the Cost of Capital and works towards maximization of Shareholder wealth. The following services are provided by Merchant Banks in this regard, namely, Optimum Capital Structure is determined as well as getting consent from the Controller of Capital to issue Bonus Shares by the capitalization of Reserves.

Issue Management and Underwriting

Issue Management and underwriting involve management activities around public issues of corporate securities, namely, equity shares, preference shares, bonds, and debentures to procure money from the Capital Market. SEBI Guidelines are followed in regard to issue management and underwriting.

Portfolio Management

Portfolio Management involves investment decisions in marketable securities with minimum risks. Merchant Bankers provide advice on select investments, collect, and remit dividends and interests, undertake any investment in securities, and provide safe custody of securities in India and overseas.

Working Capital Finance

Merchant Bankers do Working capital finance which is the fund required for the day-to-day expenses of the enterprise. They assess working capital requirements and facilitate the sanction of credit facilities for speedy disbursements.

Mergers, Amalgamations, and Takeover

For Mergers, Amalgamations, and Takeovers, Merchant Bankers arrange for the negotiation of acquisitions and mergers by offering expert valuation services. They also conduct a SWOT analysis, and studies for locating overseas markets, foreign collaborations, and joint ventures. This is done after getting approvals from shareholders and stakeholders and monitoring the implementation of amalgamations and any major mergers.

Venture Capital and Lease Financing

Venture Capital is the seed capital in the form of equity financing for high-risk and high-reward projects. Leasing is a fund-based financial service where leasing let the lessee uses assets for a particular period of time. The services provided are for giving advice on the feasibility of leasing as well as providing advice on a rental structure.

Code of Conduct

The Code of Conduct stipulates the duties of a Merchant Banker which include acting in an ethical manner, informing clientele that the Merchant Banker is obliged to follow the Code of Conduct, exercising due diligence, no-involvement in unfair practices, having no misrepresentations, always providing good advice, etc.

The Merchant Banker is also supposed to abide by all the rules and regulations, guidelines, and resolutions passed by the Government of India and SEBI at all times.

4

Operating Procedures of Monetary Policy in India

In this lesson, Day-to-day management of monetary conditions that make up the overall calibre of Monetary Policy, which is called Operating Procedures of Monetary Policy is discussed.

Generally, the Operating Procedures of Monetary Policy involve,

- o An Operational target whereby a particular operational target is chosen in order to achieve that target or work around it.
- o For that purpose, the Central Bank plans different money market operations in a way that is distinct in its nature, extent, and frequency.
- o To calibrate short-term market rates, a corridor is used and a specific width is recommended and,
- o a specific way of signalling policy intentions.

Now let us explain what are the Operating Procedures of Monetary Policy in India.

Liquidity Adjustment Facility
(LAF)
A Liquidity Adjustment Facility (Narasimhan Committee) is a tool of the Monetary Policy, primarily from RBI, that allows a bank to borrow money at the REPO rate from

the Reserve Bank of India and to lend money or make a loan to the RBI using Reverse REPO arrangements.

LAF by increasing or decreasing the money supply can manage inflation in the economy.

Various banks use securities as collateral by making a repo agreement and use the cash, which is loan given to bank by RBI for their short-term requirements and remain stable in the market.

The transactions of liquidity adjustment facility take place at a particular time in a day. Generally, an entity who has shortfalls in cash, engages in repo agreements and an entity who has excess cash engages in Reverse repo agreements.

Whenever RBI reduces the REPO rate, the bank borrows which would mean there will be excess cash in the system, prompting the bank to lend money to the borrowers. This in turn would increase economic activity in the system.

Overnight, when the bank agrees to buy back the securities from RBI by offering a loan, it is done at the reverse repo rate, which also stands reduced, whenever there is any such move by the country's Central Bank.

For Policy Rate, in a surplus liquidity condition, the reverse repo rate becomes the operating policy rate and in a deficit liquidity situation, the repo rate becomes the policy rate, though in international best practices, it is highly unlikely to have two policy rates. Bank Rate was used as an instrument of Monetary Control until LAF system was instituted and progressively facilities for refinance were provided at repo rate.

Nowadays, Bank Rate is used as a penalty whenever there is a default in CRR and SLR as required by the RBI and BR (Banking Regulations) Act.

Monetary Policy Corridor

(MPC)

MPC is one of the instruments that RBI has introduced in its monetary policy toolkit where it indicates an area between two rates of RBI's Monetary Policy which is at the lowest level, Reverse Repo rate and at the ceiling lies MSF (Marginal Standing Facility) Rate.

Reverse Repo rate will be the lowest of the policy rates and MSF rate will be the ceiling more than Repo rate.

The Reverse Repo rate and the MSF rate determine the corridor in the weighted average call money rate for all the daily movements.

In the recent episode of liquidity tightness, the RBI has been providing additional liquidity up to 2 percent of Net Demand and Time Liabilities, at the repo rate, mostly on an ad hoc basis. The advantages exist because it provides an upper bound to the policy rate corridor. It will also provide a safety valve against unprecedented liquidity shocks.

In a liquidity deficit situation, it will help stabilize the overnight interest rate around repo and it will enhance the liquidity attribute of the SLR portfolio. The width of the corridor should be in such a manner that it should be narrow enough to induce volatility in short term money market rates and it should be wide enough so that it does not stunt the development of short-term money market especially by taking away the incentive from market participants so that they deal amongst themselves before approaching the central bank.

Operating Target

The operating target of the Monetary Policy is the overnight call money rate, as the monetary transmission in this segment is the fastest. However, it is noticed that in the past few years, the turnover in the uncollateralized segment has reduced sharply in the inter-bank money market segment.

But the turnover has increased in Collateralized Borrowing and Lending Obligations and Market Repo.

This may seem to suggest that the prudential limits prescribed by the RBI have not constrained the growth of Call Money Market rather it increased the money market and its stability, with an increased share of the collateralized segment. Before we let you go, it is equally important that we see the significance of Monetary Transmission. In other words, Operating Procedures pay special attention to Monetary Transmissions and Policy Rates. This is what we explain next.

Monetary Transmissions and Channels

Monetary Policy actions through changes in financial prices and financial quantities are transmitted to the rest of the economy.

Financial prices are mostly interest rates, exchange rates and yields along with equity prices and asset prices. Financial Quantities are essentially foreign dominated assets, government bonds, money supply, and credit aggregates.

Sometimes due to concerns in Money Demand Function, increased attention is thrown to Financial Price Channel. In particular, the Interest Rate channel emerges as the key channel of transmission, mostly because short term interest rates emerge as a predominant instrument of worldwide monetary signals.

An increase in nominal short term interest rate gives way to higher real interest rates.

This is seen to affect the investment and spending behaviours of firms as well as the individuals. For them, the disposable income is reduced and the current consumption from the perspective of market is reduced. However, the savings behaviour gathers momentum and more people starts to save in the society. Also, the higher interest rate is seen to diminish the profit of firms.

This in turn would signal that new investments are less attractive. In other words, consumption and investment reduces which typically shrinks output. This in turn would pull the prices of goods downwards.

As prices of goods and wages adjust in the long run, real GDP will be in the potential level where real interest rate and real exchange rate returns to their fundamental levels.

Methods of Credit Control

Introduction to Credit Control

The Reserve Bank of India is always faced with the dual problems of ensuring price stability in the event of a steep increase in money supply arising out of a sudden expansion of credit as well as making provisions for financing economic growth.

The effectiveness of Monetary Policy then is questioned due to increased public expenditure and the subsequent rise in bank deposits.

Hence, the Reserve Bank is forced to adopt a balancing approach taking refuge in a policy of controlled expansion of credit, meeting the objectives of ensuring price stability as well as making provisions for credit for the attainment of faster economic growth.

In this context, we will examine the two most important methods of Credit Control namely,

- o Quantitative Methods of Credit Control and,
- o Qualitative Methods of Credit Control.

In this session, we will discuss Qualitative Methods of Credit Control.

Qualitative Methods of Credit Control

Qualitative Methods are used by RBI for selective purposes in Credit Control. Some of the important ones are,

- Consumer Credit Regulations: This is for issuing of rules regarding the maximum maturity of installment credit and down payments for goods and for the purchase of goods. Down payment is increased or decreased based on inflation or depression in the economy.
- Margin Requirements are the differences between the amount borrowed by banks and securities offered. While granting of a loan by the bank, it is RBI's prescription to the bank to maintain a percentage of the margin. During inflation, RBI will increase the margin, so that only less money will be there with the borrower and this may affect the borrowing capacity and demand for goods. Margin will be reduced in the case of Depression.
- Credit Rationing: In Credit Rationing, RBI controls the credit granted or allocated by the Commercial banks. This distribution of credit will be done according to the national economy's conditions. More demand in one sector will fix a percentage of loans in relation to total advances.
- Direct Action: To banks who do not fulfill requirements and conditions, this action will be taken by the RBI. RBI may give excess credits or charge a penal rate of interest above the Bank rate or may even refuse to rediscount papers if the credit demanded is beyond a certain limit.

6

Quantitative Methods of Credit Control

In this section, we will elaborate on the Quantitative Method of Credit Control.

Quantitative Methods of Credit Control

Quantitative Methods of Credit Control involve the following controls namely,

- o Bank Rate Policy,
- o Open Market Operations and
- o Variable Reserve Ratios and Rates namely, Cash Reserve Ratio, Statutory Liquidity Ratio, Repo Rate as well as Reverse Repo Rate.

Bank Rate Policy

The official interest rate at which RBI rediscounts bills in particular approved bills that are held by the commercial bank is called the Bank Rate. This naturally, controls the money supply, credit, and inflation, whenever the RBI increases the Bank Rate.

How does it work?

The way it works is that whenever the RBI increases the Bank Rate, Commercial banks will have to pay a higher rate of interest for their loans from the RBI. This increased rate is passed on to the borrowers of the bank by the Commercial banks and hence there will be fewer people borrowing money from commercial banks. This means, naturally borrowers will be discouraged to borrow from commercial banks. This in turn would reduce trading and business activities which will reduce the price level and money supply in the country's economy.

Open Market Operations
(OMO)

OMO is the direct purchase and sale of bills and securities in the Open Market by the RBI. The volume of credit as a result will get controlled. Also, by selling in the money market, excess money supply with financial institutions, commercial banks, and insurance companies will be absorbed by the RBI.

What happens during inflation is that the commercial banks will be encouraged to buy the securities that RBI sells in the Market. Thus, surplus cash with commercial banks will be left with fewer amounts of funds, which will in turn reduces borrowing as banks cannot borrow money out which brings down the economic activity in the country.

Variable Ratio and Rates
The following ratio and rates are discussed.

- o Cash Reserve Ratio: It is that portion of total deposits in the Commercial bank that has to be left with RBI as Cash Reserves. If CRR is reduced, more money will be there with the Commercial banks based on that they increase the borrowing activity increasing economic activities.

- o Statutory Liquidity Ratio: It is that portion of deposits with the banks that must be kept as liquid assets (cash, gold, approved government securities). This helps RBI to control banks' money supplies.
- o Repo Rate: It is the rate at which RBI lends money to the banks or banks borrow from the RBI against approved securities.
- o Reverse Repo Rate: This is the rate at which Banks lend money to RBI or RBI obtains loans from the Commercial Banks.

Security Market Operations

7

An Introduction to Funds from International Markets

Introduction

A well-established and efficiently functioning Financial Market is a must for a country that is undergoing massive economic development.

Indian Economic System is reconstituted in the backbone of Industrial Deregulation, Liberalization of policies relating to FDI (Foreign Direct Investment), Reforms in the Public Enterprise Sector, Trade liberalization, and Financial Sector Reforms after 1992.

Whenever we speak about Financial Sector reforms, we stress three important factors: Commercial Banking, Capital Markets, and Non-Banking Finance Companies.

Here we attempt to study the contributions made by the Global Financial market in the backdrop of the years of development we experience, after the implementation of Liberalization Policies in 1992 and of the laying out of a large proportion of resources required for investment from the public and private sectors and even from the Capital Markets.

International Financial Markets

International Financial Markets or Global Financial Markets are markets that operate outside of the regulations, domain, and legislative framework of our country, India. However, it is more than equally likely that Global Capital Transactions may take place in domestic Capital Markets within a country.

Constituents of Global Financial Markets

It is already understood that the operations of the Global Financial Market are not subject to the rules and regulations of a particular country. An example cited in this case may be Euro Bonds issued by a syndicate of International banks and is constantly placed under the control of investors and lenders from all over the world.

When we analyse the Global Financial Markets, we can say that it is made up of,

- o Euro Currency Market
- o International Bond Market
- o Institutional Finance and
- o Export Credit Facilities.

In this session, we will briefly take a look at what each of them means.

Euro Currency Market

Following World War II, the market was pounded with Euro Dollar Deposits in the form of Bank Deposits, and Loans and this market later became the Euro Currency Market. The basis of the Euro Currency Market lies in the fact that Banks in Europe accept dollar-denominated deposits and give dollar-denominated loans to the Customers of the numerous European Banks. This Euro Currency Market was popular in Europe, particularly in London, after World War II.

International Bond Market

International Bond Market or otherwise known as the Euro Bond Market existed in Europe and with the help of this, long-term funds were raised using different types of underlying instruments. We will explain more about this as we progress our learning on Euro Currency Market.

Institutional Finance

International Finance Institutions that provide finance in Foreign Currency make up Institutional Finance. Examples include, IMF or the International Monetary Fund, World Bank and its aligned agencies like International Finance Corporation, Asian Development Bank, etc.

Export Credit facilities

Credit facilities for international business are constituted under an institutional framework known as EXIM Banks in certain countries including India. Export Credit facilities are mainly provided by the EXIM Bank. In that regard, EXIM bank plays a major role in conducting off shore deals and in the financing of exports.

Instruments used in International Market for raising funds

In International Market, the instruments used for raising funds are US Dollar, Euro, Pound Sterling, Deutsche Mark, Swiss Francs, and Canadian Dollars.

Canadian Dollars appeared in the World Market in the year 1975 and the issue of Canadian Dollar Euro Bonds became attractive for International Borrows. It was attractive for investors because it was cheaper than other currencies in circulation for international trade then and because of its ease of convertibility to other currencies.

50

FII Investments

What are FII (Foreign Institutional Investor) Investments?

A Foreign Institutional Investor means an institution that is incorporated or established outside India and proposes to make an investment in India, mainly in Securities is deemed an FII.

Also, a Domestic Asset Management Company or a Domestic Portfolio Manager who manages funds that are raised or collected or brought from outside of India for investment in India on behalf of a subaccount is also deemed as an FII.

The SEBI Regulations that govern Foreign Institutional Investment in India fall under the classes,

- General Obligations and Responsibilities,
- Investment Conditions and Restrictions,
- Registration of FII including subaccounts,
- Action or Penalty in case of Default, and
- Preferential allotment by listed companies to FII.

In this list, we define registration of FII including Subaccounts first and then go defining the other classes.

Registration of FII with SEBI

For buying, selling, and dealing in securities, FII must register with SEBI (Securities and Exchange Board of India).

The Certificate of Registration is granted to an FII after it considers the following matters, namely,

- Applicant FII's Financial Performance, Applicant FII's Professional Capacity, Applicant FII's Financial Strength, Applicant FII's General Reputation of Fairness and Integrity is considered before granting of Certificate of Registration,
- Applicant FII will be subject to regulation by an appropriate foreign regulatory authority,
- Applicant FII must obtain other permissions under FEMA by RBI for making investment in the capacity of an FII,
- The FII Applicant should be established or incorporated outside of India as a Pension Fund, Mutual Fund, Investment Trust, or Asset Management Company.
- FII Applicant must have been in existence for the past 5 years.

All these conditions have to be satisfied by the FII Applicant for them to be legally permitted to invest in securities outside their country of incorporation.

Investment Conditions and Restrictions

SEBI has permitted FIIs to invest in Securities of the Indian Capital Market according to the provisions listed as under,

- Investment is permitted in primary and secondary markets and this includes investment in shares, debentures, warrants of listed, unlisted, or to-be-listed companies on a recognized Stock Exchange in India,

- o Investment is permitted in units of Mutual Funds, Unit Trust of India whether listed, or not,
- o Investment is permitted in Commercial Papers, and
- o Investment in Dated Government securities.

An FII must apply for a renewal certificate for renewal three months before the expiry of the Certificate of Registration.

Preferential Allotment by Listed Companies to FII

SEBI has granted permission to Listed Companies in order to make a preferential allotment to Registered FII under the following conditions,

- o The Companies making preferential allotment to Registered FII must secure or obtain the consent of the Shareholders after conducting Annual General Body Meeting,
- o The Preferential Allotment made to each FII should be within limits, within ceiling on FII Holdings, and
- o Price fixation to be made should be not less than highest price during the last 26 weeks on all the stock exchanges.

This completes an overview on FII Investments...

Euro Issues

Issuers across the world were interested in expanding capital markets so that their investor base is increased and they felt the possibility of raising equity and debt as an omnipresent scenario, not limited at least by geography. At the same time, investor increasingly diversified their holding so that their yields remain increased.

This led to the emergence of a Global Financial Market that spread across national boundaries and started to encourage cross-border capital flows to, those who were seeking low-cost funding, from those who have funds but were searching for higher returns.

Indian companies were allowed to access International Equity Market, consequently, after the Economic Liberalization that happened in 1991 as well as the New Economic Policy that was instrumental in the same year.

Though for a long time, Indian Companies were issuing in the Debt Capital Markets, mainly, Floating Rates Notes and Fixed Rates Bonds (Yankee Bonds), issues in International Capital Markets in the Indian Context were a recent phenomenon, mainly in the form, of Euro Issues which are, Global Depository Receipts (GDR) and Foreign Currency Convertible Bonds (FCCB). In this session, we will explain Euro Issues, mainly, Global Depository Receipts and FCCB.

Global Depository Receipts

Depository Receipts were created long before 1930 in the United States so that US Investors could purchase shares of Non-US Corporations. This mechanism and structure were so popular in the US that it was used by issuers to access investors worldwide and was used as a mechanism to raise equity outside of the US home market.

Identified on the basis of the market where each of the Depository Receipts served in the US during 1933, they were classified into,

- American Depository Receipts which were available to US Investors indicated by American,
- Rule 144A DR which was privately placed to a select group of investors according to Rule 144A of the Securities Act 1933, and
- Global Depository Receipts.

In this session, we will only go through Global Depository Receipts (GDR).

GDR

Global Depository Receipts are Depository Receipts offered to investors in markets that are outside the US, the country where it is issued and offered through a Global rendering. The offering made in the case of Global Depository Receipts is made according to a Rule 144A of the Securities Act while issuing to all investors within the US and when offered to Asia/Europe and

Latin America, it is offered within the framework of Regulation S of the Securities Act.

GDR Issuing Mechanism

GDR is a negotiable certificate evidencing ownership in the shares of a foreign corporation, where the foreign corporation is from a country outside the market in which GDRs are traded. With GDR, foreign companies can trade in the stock exchanges of any country except the stock exchange of the US.

Normally GDRs are issued, when the foreign Company, foreign to US, let us say an Indian Company (hereafter foreign means anything outside India) delivers Ordinary Equity Shares issued in the name of an overseas or Foreign as in a US depository bank to an Indian Custodian, who holds the shares as an agent of the Foreign Depository Bank, who by then would issue receipts called Global Depository Receipts representing those ordinary shares with the Indian Custodian, to an overseas customer or investor.

Which currency are they traded in?

GDR is traded in the currency of the country they trade in and are quoted. They are governed by settlement and trading procedures of the market in which they are traded in and are quoted. They may be denominated in any currency but generally US Dollars.

What makes them attractive?

GDR is eligible for book-entry settlements in the US through Depository Trust Company and in Europe through Cedel, Euroclear, and European Settlement System. Settlements of International Trade using GDR are much faster when compared to trade in the Indian system and this makes them a very attractive investment option for investors from foreign countries willing to purchase shares.

Advantages

To the issuer, it enables, access to markets that are broader and deeper outside the home market and enables raising capital at a much better price. It also enhances company visibility and expands the shareholder base.

To the Investor, it eliminates custody charges, it permits deals to be done in US Dollars and supports diversification into foreign securities.

Rights of a GDR Holder

Like the holder of an underlying equity share, the GDR Holder has the right to receive dividends and bonuses upon declaration and also has access to Rights Issues. GDR Holder can always direct the Foreign Depository on how to vote, even though they may not have direct voting rights. The fungibility of GDR which measures the extent to which GDR and equity shares are interchangeable is partial in India. Hence, the company does not have the right to convert GDR and release Equity shares to be sold to international investors, although the Indian government is considering a move to support the two-way fungibility of Global Depository Receipts in India.

Indian Scenario

Exciting opportunities are provided by India for international investors through Foreign Institutional investment and through the mechanism of GDR. However, Foreign Institutional Investor has regulatory restrictions on what they can invest in, in India, whereas

GDR is almost considered by the issuing company as direct foreign investment.

In India, the issue of GDR is as per norms set by the Ministry of Finance, Government of India. The permission to float GDR is provided by the Department of Economic Affairs, Ministry of Finance, if the company has a track record of good performance consistently for 3 years.

Foreign Currency Convertible Bonds (FCCB)

A Foreign Currency Convertible Bond is an unsecured debt instrument that is equity linked carrying a fixed rate of interest with an option to convert into GDR of the issuer company or a fixed number of equity shares for domestic investors. They are traded after listing on one or more stock exchanges abroad. The interest is paid in US Dollars or any other currency that is freely convertible until the conversion is made on the FCCB.

The main advantage of FCCB is while raising funds it helps in deferring the dilution of capital until conversion and this is definitely an advantage for the issuer.

Usually, FCCBs are structured with a call option for the issuer to call the bond after a specified period subject to the domestic share price exceeding the conversion price or a certain percentage of the conversion price.

It is said FCCB has a dismal performance at the time when it was first introduced in the Indian Market.

10

Pricing of GDR

The Actual Process

Indian Issuers use the Book Building method as a common and effective method of offering securities in the international market. In this method, the preliminary offering document is Red-Herring by the issuer which marks the beginning of the Book Building Process.

As a process, first, the marketing of securities is done, and then the offer price of the securities is determined. Afterwards, the Finalization of the offer document is made based on the previous steps.

On the basis of the Offer Document, the Global coordinator or Bookrunner who is the Investment Bank managing the Issue acts through a network of Managers called Syndicate Members, and assesses the level of interest in the demand for GDR that gets offered.

On a non-binding basis, the prospective investors indicate whether they would be interested in acquiring GDR and convey the price at which such an acquisition may be made possible.

This is the Book of Demand and is made by the Investment Bank which is built over a period of one to two weeks during which time, marketing of the issue takes place which is also known as Roadshows. Group Presentations are made on those Roadshows to the investors by the company management and separate meetings are held with them mostly on a one-to-one basis.

At the end of the Book Building Period depending upon the Level of Demand, the price of the GDR issue is determined. Order for the shares is then confirmed with the investor who is willing to invest in a GDR Issue.

That means, in a GDR Issue, the book-runner in consultation with the issuer decides on the shares to be allocated to the investor taking into consideration various factors or criteria.

One of the advantages of the Book Building Process is that the price of a GDR Issue is set at the end of a book-building process and is fairly accurate with the demand for shares in the market. This will in turn instil competition among investors who are now bidding on a competitive basis for shares.

After-Market Stabilization

Always After-Market stabilization is a common practice in GDR issues which is the risk which is inherent in GDR Issues, post-offer, where the demand for a GDR Issue may exceed supply or vice versa. Hence, the issuer ensures good market stabilization by providing a Green shoe option to the Lead Manager, who would over-allot and create a short position by creating more shares than whatever is available to sell.

To cover or fill such a short position, they later buy GDR from the secondary market providing adequate support to the share price, or may even purchase GDR from the issuer at the offer price.

Special Accounts

11

Factoring & Forfaiting

What is a Factor?

A Factor is an agency that makes Factoring, which is an arrangement with a business concern, which is again a financial service provided, wherein the factor undertakes the task of realizing the book debts and bill receivables of the business concern for a commission. Factor has business concerns as their clients, and undertakes to realize the debts owe to the business concern and bills receivables by making their client's debtors make payment to the client or the client's creditors. For the firms or the business concerns, Factoring helps the firm meet their working capital requirements by selling off their receivables or book debts to a Factor.

Diagrammatically,

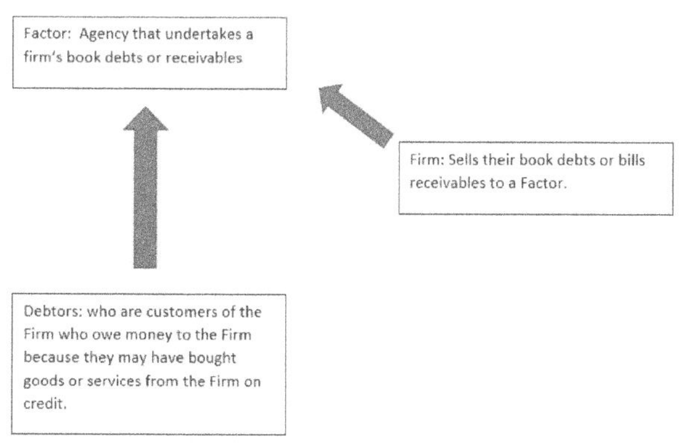

According to a report submitted to RBI, Mr. C.S. Kalyanasundaram has explained Factor as a continuous arrangement under a Financial Institution that assumes the collection functions and credit for its client by purchasing the receivables as they arise with or without recourse for credit losses and attends to other bookkeeping duties and maintains the sales ledger to such accounts and performs functions.

Explain the process followed by the Factor in the arrangement of Factoring?

Factoring involves three players, (a) Firm who sells goods or services (b) Factor which is financial institution that buys a firm's book debts or account receivables and (c) Debtors who are also a Firm's customers who owe money to the Firm because they may have bought goods or services from the firm on credit.

The following is the process of Factoring.

- o The firm gets an order of purchase of services or goods on credit through its customers
- o Firm sends invoices to their customer or debtors and also sends goods or performs service and then the firm informs the customer or directs its debtors that the invoice assigned to the customer should be paid to a Factor.
- o Firm also sends the customer invoice to the factor which is a valid proof of credit sales and dispatch.
- o Factor by buying the book debts or accounts receivable prepays the firm to the extent 90 % of the invoice value
- o Factor follows up with the customer for realization of the payment due.

- o Debtor pays the money to the factor on due date or in other words, the factor collects book debts.
- o Factor after collecting money from the customers does pay the balance of the invoice value to the firm.

What is Forfaiting?

Forfaiting In French means to surrender one's rights on something to someone and is a popular form of financing of account receivables arising out of international trade. This is done by discounting export receivables by taking proper evidence on matters like bill of exchange or promissory notes without recourse to the exporter carrying long-term maturities to medium on a fixed rate which is 100% of contract value. Forfaiting is extended to export of capital goods, services, or commodities where the exporter may insist on supplies on credit terms.

In Forfaiting there are four parties in a transaction and are Exporter, Importer, Importer's bank (Guarantor), and Discounting Bank (Forfeiter).

Briefly explain the process of forfaiting?

The process of Forfaiting is where,

- o There exists a proposed exports sales contract between an exporter and an importer (b) The importer approaches his local bank to issue Letter of Credit which is a Guarantee in support of Promissory Notes or Bill of Exchange in favour of the exporter.
- o The Exporter approaches the Forfeiter (Discounting Bank) to establish terms of Forfeiting.

- o The forfeiter (Discounting Bank) quotes the discount rate after estimating risk
- o The Exporter sells goods
- o Importer draws Promissory note in favour of exporter
- o Exporter draws bill and gets acceptance of the importer
- o The Exporter enters into a forfeiting agreement with the forfeiter or discounting bank
- o Exporter sells bills or notes to the forfeiter at discount
- o Forfeiter (Discounting Bank) presents the bill to the importer for payment on the due date or may sell the bill in the capital market.

What are the salient features of Forfaiting?

The salient features of forfaiting are,

- o Forfaiting is used to finance only export business
- o It involves export bill and purchase of export bill
- o It is mainly towards single transaction backed by a Bank guarantee or a Letter of Credit '
- o It is both long term or medium-term financing with credit period that extend from 180 days to 7 years.
- o The exporter must manage the export receivables account because a forfeiter's (Discounting bank's) responsibility extends to the collection of forfeited debt only.
- o The transaction should be of minimum value of USD 2,50,000.
- o The Forfeiter may realize the export bill in the securities market or hold onto it until due date.

12

Lead Managers

Introduction
What is a Syndicate?
Who can act as Lead Manager to an Issue?

A Syndicate is a group of underwriters who are responsible for the placement of securities in a new issue with the investors and is a temporary arrangement. In a Syndicate, what is subordinated to the Managing Underwriter is the underwriting firm itself. The lead manager is assigned a part of the new placement issue, and it may be the second largest part.

By SEBI Regulations, only Merchant Bankers who are category I can act as Lead Managers to an Issue.

More SEBI Guidelines
The following SEBI Guidelines are followed in fixing the number of Lead Managers to an Issue.

- o   If the issue is less than Rs. 50 crores, the number of lead managers can only be at the maximum two.
- o   If the issue is between 50 crores and less than Rs. 100 crores, the maximum number of lead managers to that issue cannot exceed three.
- o   Between Rs. 100 crores and Rs. 200 crores, the number of Lead Managers cannot exceed 4 and

for sizes above Rs. 200 crores less than 400 crores, the number of Lead Managers cannot exceed five.
- o For any size above Rs. 400 crores, the number of Lead Managers can be more than 5 as may be again stipulated by SEBI.

Some of the conditions that are applicable in the case of Registration or Renewal certification are,

- o After a change in conditions, prior approval of SEBI is necessary to continue to act as a Merchant Banker.
- o Within one month of the complaint, if there are any, Merchant Bankers should take adequate steps to re-address investor grievances.

Responsibilities of Lead Manager

Merchant Bankers should give a statement that should be included in an agreement with SEBI specifying the details of the Issue for the subscription. It should be sent to SEBI at least one month prior to the opening of the issue for subscription and the statement should contain details of all Lead Managers and their responsibilities. The undertaking obligation accepted by Lead Manager is 5% of the total underwriting commitment or Rupees 25 lakhs whichever is lesser.

A due diligence certificate should be filed by Lead Manager to SEBI two weeks before the issue is opened for subscription. It should state that the prospectus or letter of offer is in full agreement with all materials or documents which are produced and in relevance to the issue for the subscription.

The disclosures made in the documents which are stated above should be true and fair and should enable investors to take decisions regarding investment where the documents should be in legal compliance including all legal requirements in connection to the documents so submitted.

Responsibilities of Merchant Banker

The Merchant Banker must submit to SEBI the following particulars of the issue including a Draft Prospectus and other literature to be circulated to investors or shareholders two weeks before the date of filing of issues for the subscription.

Filing Fee

The Merchant Banker should file a flat rate of Rupees 25,000 up to Rupees 10 crores and between Rupees 10 crore and 5000 crores 0.025% of the issue size and beyond would be 1.25 crore plus 0.00625% of the issue size. For Rights issues, up to Rupees 10 crores, it is a flat rate of Rupees 25,000 from Rupees 10 crore to Rupees 500 crore it is 0.005% of issue size and for more than Rupees 500 crore, it is a flat charge of Rupees 5 lakhs.

Business Restrictions

Lead Manager should not agree to manage any issues unless his responsibilities of Disclosures, Allotment, and Refund are clearly defined relating to the Issues for Subscription. A statement to that effect should be furnished to SEBI.

Global Financial Management

13

Transaction Exposure

Introduction to Currency Risk

From the relative valuation of currencies, emerge Currency Risk. This is where changes result in unpredictable losses or gains, where the changes themselves involve an investment's profits and dividends converted into foreign currencies.

Here also, investors reduce currency risk by using hedges which are designed to offset many currency-related losses or gains.

Here also, a typical illustration may be a trader buying German stocks for let us say 10 euros. After this purchase, if the Euro depreciates in exchange rate from 1.5 USD to 1.3 USD, the investor when he sells the German stock is believed to realize a 13% loss on the transaction, unless he hedges it using a Forward Contract or Option, as explained under topic, Hedging Adverse Price Movements using Options.

Currency Risks

Ideally, there are three different types of Currency Risks and are namely,

- Transaction Exposure,
- Translation Exposure, and Economic Exposure.

Let us explain in some detail what each of them means.

Transaction Exposure

This is the risk that is encountered when the firm engages in commercial transactions where the currency of the transaction is foreign. For managing this risk, we use hedging with Money market hedges. The other methods may be hedging with, Futures, Forwards, and Options (See section under Hedging Adverse Price Movements using Options).

Money Market Hedge

This method is also called by the name, Synthetic Forward Contract. In this method, it uses a combination of Call Option and Put Option at the same strike price which this Money Market Hedge is going to hedge. This would mean the combination of Call Option and Put Option will be at the same strike price at the same time to expiry to create an offsetting position in the event there is a currency or an exchange risk. There is a net optimum premium that the Money Market Hedge investor needs to pay to the seller which is in fact a premium to compensate for the seller's obligation upon the buyer's or investor's right to sell an option or buy it.

Now for illustration purposes, let us consider a Money Market Hedge which is a Synthetic Long Forward Contract on XYZ Inc Stock at a $40 strike price for June 30, 2023.

- o In order to create that, an Investor should buy a call with $40 strike price with an expiry on June 30, 2023.
- o Also, an investor writes a Put Option with a $40 strike price with expiry on June 30, 2023.
- o If the stock price on 30th June 2023 is above the strike price on the expiration date, the investor

does call at the strike price so that he can buy cheap the stock on 30th June 2023.

- o If the stock price on 30th June 2023 is below the strike price on the expiration date, the investor does put (sell) the stock at the strike price so that he earns a lot more money than the stock price and then would again use that money to buy a greater number of stocks on 30th June 2023.

In both cases, the investor would end up buying the stock at the strike price which is locked in with the synthetic Long Forward Contract on 30th June 2023.

Managing Transactional Exposure using Operational Techniques

Adopting operational strategies and techniques that have the power to offsetting existing foreign currency exposure, the Operational techniques are effective in places where there are no forward contracts or futures available for a particular currency chosen.

The Strategies are, Sharing Currency Risk, Risk Shifting, Reinvoice centres, and Leading and Lagging.

Sharing Currency Risk

Sharing of currency risk among two parties to a transaction is an effective way currency risk is shared. It works on the principle that; one party's loss is another party's gain. Usually, this adjustment works on the premise that any change in the exchange rate from the agreed rate on the date of the transaction will be split between two parties that are on either end of a transaction. By working and selecting on a bare spot rate, the adjustment yields avoidance of currency risk for a particular transaction in question, by sharing the loss and gains resulting from such currency transactions.

Risk Shifting

Obviously, the only way to reduce the exposure is not to have an exposure by itself.

Now how this can be done?

By invoicing to the extent possible all transactions in home currency, a firm avoids transaction exposure altogether. But this would not work for everyone, since dealing with a foreign currency sometimes becomes inevitable. In such cases, a firm is made responsible to bear all the currency risk wherever foreign currency is involved and this is by making sure the firm chosen does it at the lowest cost.

Reinvoice Centres

It is a corporate subsidiary managing in a location all transaction exposure from the trade that emerges out of intra-company activities. Here the manufacturing centre sells goods to foreign distributor affiliates through a re-invoicing centre. The main difference is that in the re-invoicing centre, the affiliate transactions are carried out in the affiliate's local currency and also the reinvoicing centre absorbs all the transaction exposure.

Leading and Lagging

Playing with the lead and lag times is one other way currency exposure is avoided. This is done by first lowering the gains and losses in currency transactions by playing with the timing of foreign currency cash flows. Leading is when if the foreign currency in which an existing nominal contract is denominated is appreciating, liabilities then are paid off and the receivables are taken in later.

Lagging is just the opposite where coincidental indicators are looked back or past transactions are analysed to know about trends in the future.

14

Translation Exposure

What is Translation Exposure?

Also called as Accounting Exposure or Balance Sheet Exposure, Translation Exposure is the restatement of Foreign Currency Financial Statements in terms of a reporting currency and this exposure is there because of a periodic need to report consolidated operations of a group that may be worldwide in one reporting currency.

This process also gives out the Financial Position of a group, having foreign subsidiaries, in the Reporting Currency which might be the local currency where the group of companies' function.

When Translation Exposure is measured?

Translation Exposure of a group is measured when translating the financial statements of its foreign subsidiary into local currency or reporting currency for reporting purposes. It is highly indicative of the possibility of gains or losses as a result of the Translations that are effective for converting as per an Exchange rate of the foreign operations of a group.

Due to such translations of foreign operations of a group or a foreign subsidiary, the gains or losses may be reversed in future accounting periods but do not represent realized cash flows unless and until the group is liquidated in whole or part or the assets and liabilities of the group get settled for the long term.

Typically, these translations do not require management action unless the management believes that translation losses or gains affect the materiality or value of a firm or business in which case it always refers to the International Accounting Standards for setting out as the best practice to be followed. These translations, also do not require management action unless certain covenants exist in the deal being formed by the group's foreign subsidiaries, for example, Gearing Profiles in a Loan Agreement that may be breached as a result of the translation to domestic currency position.

When does a firm experience Translation Exposure?

A firm experiences or is subjected to Translation Exposure when it has subsidiaries or assets in a foreign country.

Translation Exposure happens as a result of the consequence of the fact that a parent company must consolidate all its operations including the operations of its foreign subsidiary into its own financial statement in a reporting currency, which most likely is the local currency of the parent firm.

Why is Translation Exposure also called as Accounting Exposure?

Fluctuating exchange rates may result in losses or gains during the translation process and as a result, this type of exposure will immediately relate to the Balance Sheet's Assets and Liabilities, one reason why this type of translation exposure is also called as Accounting Exposure.

Illustration of Translation Exposure

Before any discussions on Translation Exposure, we have to also keep in mind that in general a firm or company that has a foreign subsidiary, quite often prefers to do the Translation based on an Exchange Rate that is Current or of Historic value.

For illustration purposes, let us consider a US Company that has a Mexican subsidiary and the subsidiary buys an asset for 12 million pesos. Considering the inflation rate of Mexico to be 50% and that of US to be 0%, and considering the purchasing parity holds, the exchange rate for 1 year is considered 18 pesos per USD.

So, applying Historical cost accounting, the asset will have a value of 12 million pesos in the Mexican subsidiary's books but while translating at 18 pesos (150 % considering inflation) per USD, the US Dollar value is estimated to be 12,000,000/18=666,667 USD.

> Translating historical cost of 12 Million pesos at historical exchange rate at the time of acquisition that is 12 pesos/USD, the USD Dollar equivalent of Asset is 12,000,000/12=1,000,000 USD.

Thus, the correct value to be used is historical exchange rate when books are kept at historical cost basis.

> Also, considering Mexico, as a country that utilizes inflation-adjusted (current) accounting system, the assets indexed will be adjusted to 18,000,000 pesos (150% considering inflation of 50%) and translating using current exchange rate of 18 pesos/USD yields, 18,000,000/18=1,000,000 USD.

If the historical exchange rate is used, the amount equivalent would be, 18,000,000/12=1,500,000 USD.

Hence it is to be surmised that for proper translation of value, we should either use the current exchange rate with current accounting practices or we should use the historical exchange rate with historical cost accounting.

Translation Exposure – Measuring

In short, the translation exposure measures the aftereffects of an exchange rate on published financial statements of a firm where we consider the translations based on Assets and Liabilities held by a firm (Balance Sheet).

For that purpose, we say,

- o What remains unexposed are assets & Liabilities that are translated at a historical exchange rate as they remain unaffected by exchange rate fluctuations, and
- o What remains exposed are Assets & Liabilities that are translated at the current exchange rate as the balance sheet will fluctuate in currency values over time.

And this gives way to our definition that Translation Exposure will be the difference between Exposed Assets and Exposed Liabilities.

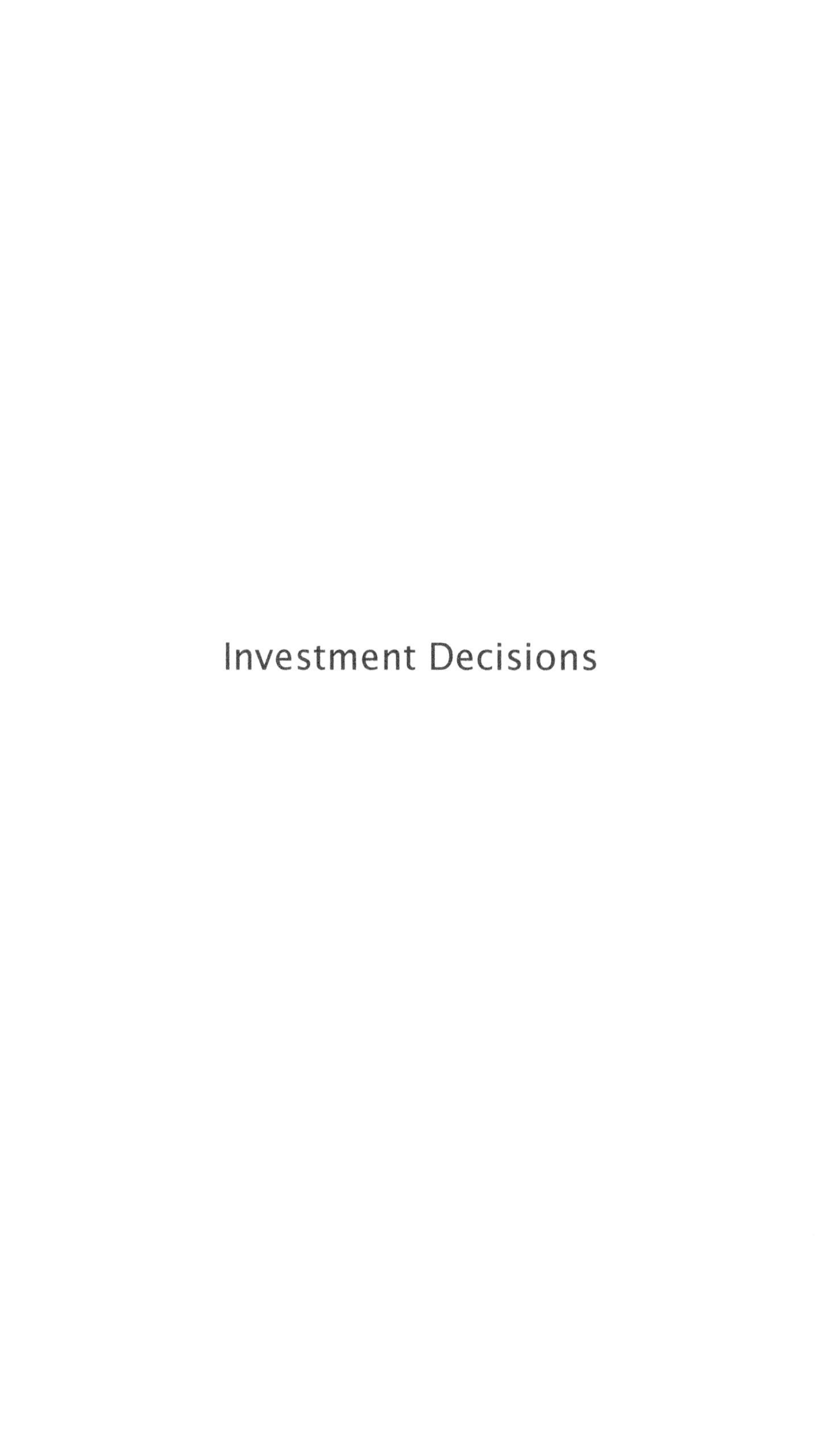

Investment Decisions

15

How to incorporate Risk into Capital Budgeting

Methods

When the financial manager makes investment decisions, under conditions where there is certainty, the investments are considered Risk free. This is the fundamental assumption of Capital Budgeting techniques, where the assumption implies for Net Present Value, whenever it is a positive value, it can be unequivocally stated that the Project Proposal remains an accepted proposal.

But in reality, that is not always true.

Due to the availability of better Technology on a day-to-day basis and due to the availability of newer and better Materials, that is Raw Materials, our estimates can get invalidated and any calculations made on the basis of for example, NPV (Net Present Value), may remain subdued or not acceptable, or in short, there exists Risk in even Capital Budgeting calculations.

So, we can say some risk is always associated with a project, so there exist cash variations and this would be reflected in every project, considered in Capital Budgeting also.

Hence, we need to basically adjust the Risk in Capital Budgeting decisions. There are two methods, it is done or taken care of; the first method being Certainty Equivalent Approach and the second method being, Risk Adjusted Discount Rate.

We will see what each of these methods means in this lesson.

Certainty Equivalent Approach

In this Approach, there are two types of Cash Flow, one is Expected Cash flow which is uncertain and the other one is Certain Cash Flow which is guaranteed to return amount on an yearly basis.

Hence the first step is finding out the Certainty Equivalent Coefficient which can be found out by two methods.

First Method of finding Certainty Equivalent Coefficient is by following $a=$(Certain Cash Flow)/(Risky Cash Flow).

Second Method of finding Certainty Equivalent Coefficient is given by the equation, Risk Premium + 1 where

Risk Premium = Risk Adjusted Rate of Return – Risk-Free Rate.

Given the Risk Premium, the Certainty Equivalent Coefficient is $a=1/((1+\text{Risk Premium}))$.

Once, a is found out, the Net Present Value is obtained by the equation, $NPV = Co + ...+(a \times Cn)/ [(1+I)]^{\wedge}n$

Calculations

The value of a varies as any value between 0 and 1.

For example, if the Expected Cash Flow is Rs. 10,08,000 and the Risk-adjusted rate of return is 12% and Risk-free Rate is 3%, the Risk Premium is calculated as 9%. Hence, $a=1/1.09=0.92$. This would mean, the Certain Cash Flow or Guaranteed Cash Flow (GCF), given the Expected Cash Flow is Rs. 10,08,000 is obtained as, GCF = 10,08,000/((1+0.09)) = Rs. 9,24,770.

Risk-Adjusted Discount Rate

In Risk-Adjusted Discount Rate, Risk is accounted for by adjusting the denominator of the NPV equation, given below, so that greater the risk, higher will be the discount value and lower will be the Net Present Value.

NPV = Co + ...+Cn/ $[(1+I)]$ ^n . Here I is adjusted.

Financial Securities

16

An Introduction to Hybrid Securities

A sort of classification for securities that combine both debt and equity characteristics and is used by a company to raise money is known as Hybrid Securities. Hybrid Securities pay a fixed or floating rate of return or dividend until a specific date in the future.

At maturity, the holder has several options including an option to convert the securities into an underlying share.

Quite in the contrary, the holder has a known cash flow if he or she owns one of the Hybrid Securities and unlike a fixed interest security, this can be converted into an underlying security or share.

Hybrid securities are in most cases structured in a unique way, where by looking at it, we may feel the price of some securities behave more like fixed interest securities whereas others behave more like underlying shares to which most of this hybrid securities can be converted.

Some of the important Hybrid Securities are,

- o   Preference Share Capital
- o   Convertible Debentures
- o   Warrants
- o   Deep Discount Bonds
- o   Secured Premium Notes and
- o   Options.

Preference Share Capital

Preference Share is a security type through which company can obtain funds in return may give preferential treatment to its preference shareholders which are not usually enjoyed by the normal equity share-holders. Preferential Share Holders enjoy a position above ordinary or equity shareholders in relation to distribution of assets, in the event of liquidation of business and in terms of income earned with respect to distribution of earnings (additional bonuses and what not).

We will explain more on this item, in a separate session on Preference Share Capital under Hybrid Securities section.

Convertible Debentures

Convertible Debentures as its name suggests is convertible to equity shares either partially or fully at a stated conversion price on a predetermined rate.

The terms of such debenture issues were fixed by the Controller of Capital Issues.

All details regarding Conversion Ratio, Conversion Premium or price and conversion timing are mentioned in the offer document or the prospectus. Conversion ratio determines the number of ordinary shares which are obtained for one convertible debenture of a particular face value. The Conversion price is the price paid for the ordinary share at the time of conversion of a fully or partially convertible Debentures.

Hence, in other words, conversion ratio is equal to par value of convertible debentures divided by conversion price. Usually, a conversion period for these debentures cannot exceed 36 months, unless the holder has the option to exercise his rights in full or in part and also there exists put and call options.

Warrants

A Warrant is an option to purchase a fixed or specific number of shares at a specified price or purchased when at the expiry of it or when there is specific time period that has elapsed. In other words, a warrant allows the holder to purchase shares of a company which is fixed in number, in future, at a fixed or pre-determined price. The holder of the warrant is allowed to sell or transfer his right in the secondary market or he or she is allowed to keep his or her right on the instrument as an investment. If the holder of the warrant exercises the option, the investor becomes a share holder in the usual or normal way. The investor who exercises the option sends the required cash and warrants to the issuing company, where the company upon receipt of the documents, issues shares.

Deep Discount Bonds

A Deep Discount Bond is a zero-interest bond and it is not convertible. Even though, a deep discount bond has a face value, it is usually lower or is at a discounted value. The Deep Discount Bond is redeemable at the expiry of a specific period at face value.

Secured Premium Notes

Secured Premium Notes is a tradeable instrument where the holder gets equity shares after a predetermined period of time and it has a detachable warrant, against which equity shares are released. It also has a feature of medium to long term notes.

Options

An option is a contract that gives the holder the right but not the obligation for a specific time period to buy or sell an underlying asset at a pre-determined price.

There are two types of Option, Put Option or Call option.

Call option gives the purchaser or buyer the right to buy an underlying security at a prespecified price called the strike price or exercise price, in return should pay the seller, an upfront fee known as call premium. Usually, the call premium is a negative cash flow for the buyer, unless the underlying security price goes up or goes greater than the exercise price.

Put option on the other hand, gives the option buyer the right to sell an underlying security (may be a stock) at a prespecified price to the writer or seller of the put option. In return, the buyer pays a put premium to the seller.

If the underlying stock price is less than the exercise price when the option expires, the buyer will buy the underlying stock in the stock market at less than the exercise price and immediately sell it at the exercise price of the put option.

This completes An Introduction to Hybrid Securities.

17

Preference Share Capital

Introduction

A type of security by virtue of which a company obtains funds in return for preferential treatment extended to holders of company's equity shares is called preference share capital.

The position enjoyed by the Preference Share Holders is a position above Equity Share Holders in a general preference, in income, with respect to the distribution of earnings and, in the distribution of assets, in the event of liquidation of the business.

Definitions

According to Section 85 of the Companies Act, preference shares are those shares that have a preferential right to be paid, dividends at fixed rates and have a preferential right to the return of capital in the case of liquidation of the company business.

In the case of financing, preference shares are given preference in the distribution of assets in the case of liquidation of the company business and income distribution of the company.

Preference Share is a hybrid security, possessing some elements of debt and some elements of equity, and are subordinate to all debts with respect to assets and earnings.

In Legal terms, Preference Share Capital is part of a Company's equity base and preference dividends are not tax-deductible expenses. It carries a fixed rate and fixed dividend plus preferred prior claims to assets and income, making it a resemblance to a debt.

However, it also represents an ownership interest and is never a ground for liquidation. In the case of receiving dividends, preference shareholders get it in priority over the equity shareholders. In the event of distribution of dividends, if the Director wants to pay equity dividends, then dividends to preference shareholders must be given. Theoretically, it may so happen that the company may pay only preference dividends and no dividend whatsoever to equity shareholders.

Voting Rights

According to Section 87 of the Companies Act, preference shareholders can exercise voting rights only on resolutions placed before the company and in matters concerning the rights attached to preference shares.

However, if the dividends to preference shareholders are not given, they can exercise voting right on every resolution placed before the company under conditions,

- the dividend on preference shares remains unpaid for an aggregate period of not less than 2 years and,
- in the case of cumulative preference share it remains unpaid for a period, more than 2 years and not less than 3 years.

Redemption of Preference Shares

Equity shares are not redeemable during the lifetime of the company whereas preference shares must be redeemed within a period of 20 years from the date of issue, and this is as per Section 80 A of the Companies Act.

Preference Capital is cumulative which would mean all unpaid dividends are carried forward and paid before ordinary dividends are paid.

For redemption, there are no serious penalties for breach of redemption stipulation.

The Preference Shares stated call price is normally above the issue price of shares and decreases as time goes by.

The call feature of Preference Share provides flexibility to the issuer as in the case of the call feature of the bonds. The refund of preference shares depends upon the fluctuations the market is subjected to, due to changes in interest rates, and due to the value of the preference share call feature, which is determined more or less by the same considerations.

In other words, so long as preference capital is appearing on the balance sheet, capital contributions by owners of the firm are represented, providing a security buffer to the company's creditors.

However, when the preference shares are redeemed, the funds of the company are used to redeem the preference share capital, making the security available to creditors go low by such a redemption process.

This is a cause of worry for the creditors who might have extended credit to the company based on the owner's contribution.

So, to protect creditor interest and to preserve the security available to them, Company Act Section 80 stipulates that, the redemption of preference share capital, can be redeemed out of profits that would otherwise be available for dividends and can be made out of a fresh issue of shares made for the purpose of redemption.

Also, when shares are redeemed out of distributable profits that is profits that ought to be distributed as dividends, the face value of such shares redeemed must be transferred to the Capital Redemption Reserve Account out of profits that are distributable otherwise as dividends or distributable profits.

18

Deep Discount Bonds

Concepts
A Deep Discount Bond is a bond that pays no interest, and trades in the market at a discount to its face value.

A Deep Discount Bond does not pay Coupons at periodic rates or intervals and hence, it is not subjected to reinvestment risk.

But Interest Rate Risk is valid for Deep Discount Bonds.

Perspectives from Time Value of Money
The concept of the Time Value of Money states that money that is realized today is worth more than the same denomination of money that is obtained in the future.

That is Rs. 100 today is more valuable than Rs. 100 that is obtained 1 year from now.

The reason is, one can obtain interest which is additional money, on the amount of Rs. 100 for 1 year, if the amount of Rs. 100 is obtained today rather than 1 year later.

Also, please note the formulae for finding out the price of Deep Discount Bond where the interest is calculated Annually is,

Price of the Deep Discount Bond = $\dfrac{Face\ Value}{(1+r)^n}$ where r is the interest rate and n the number of years.

That means, if Joe wants to purchase a Deep Discount Bond, with Face Value, Rs. 1000, with 5 years maturity where the interest rate is 5% compounded annually, he has to pay, 1000/(1+0.05)5 is Rs. 783.52.

Since there are no coupons which are paid by this Bond, the reinvestment risk is not there for the Bond.

But if the Interest rate goes up to say 20% on this bond, that is the next day of the day in which Joe buys the Bond, the price Joe gets if he decides to sell it is, 1000/(1+0.10)5 =Rs. 620.

So, Joe will lose money Rs. 163.52 and hence there is interest rate risk which is there in Deep Discount Bond.

So, this wraps up a short discussion of Deep Discount Bond which is also called as Zero-Coupon Bond.

Please note the bonds usually are issued by Companies whose financial standing is a question.

The idea is the more destabilized the company becomes, the interest rate on the Zero-Coupon Bond or Deep Discount Bond goes down and the seller can expect a discount by selling the Deep Discount Bond.

19

Forwards and Futures

Introduction - Forward Contract
Derivatives like Forward contracts, Options, and Swap are used for hedging underlying commodity risks, currency, and interest rates.

One thing to note is that we will restrict this discussion to Interest Rate derivatives and Currencies only.

Authorized banks take the authority to trade in Currency and Interest Rate Derivatives. However, the scene is different in the case of Futures, where individuals, other entities, and corporates freely participate in the trade involving Futures in an Exchange and not in Over the Counter or OTC.

Forward Contract
Forward Contract delivers foreign currency at a fixed exchange rate on a future date and is an OTC Product. In the case of this product, bank is always the counterparty.

(exporter)

For example, in the case of an Exporter entering into a Forward sale contract of his export proceedings denominated in USD; if he enters into a 3-month forward sale contract at Rs. 73 per dollar would mean, upon obtaining his proceeds in USD, the exporter can sell the contracted amount to the bank at Rs 73 per dollar even if the Rupee appreciates to let us say Rs. 65 per USD.

(importer)

Similarly, an importer who wants dollars is protected whenever he enters into a forward purchase contract of say Rs. 73 per dollar even if the Rupee depreciates to Rs. 78 per dollar on expiry date, which means on the expiry date, he can still get more dollars at the rate of Rs. 73 and not Rs. 78 which is the prevailing market rate.

Forward Option:

As per Contract (Forward Contract) terms, delivery of currency must be taken or given, on the expiry date of the contract, otherwise the contract may get cancelled and the difference between forward rate and spot rate will be recovered from the counterparty or credited to the counter party.

The facility where Banks allow delivery of currency to take place according to Forward Contract within a month before the expiry date is said to be called Forward Option. According to this facility, banks would quote forward premium or discount made applicable to start of end date of the option period which ever may not work to client's advantage.

Forward Rate:

Forward Rate is in fact interest rate differential of two independent currencies. To the spot rate, the forward rate is either at a premium or at a discount. Usually, the currency carrying a higher interest rate is always at a discount.

For example, since the domestic interest rate of INR is higher than the interest rate of USD, INR is always at a discount to Dollar and Dollar is at a premium to INR.

Hence, Forward rate of USD/INR is higher than the Spot Rate or always USD on a forward date is considered more rupees than what it is today. For EURO it is also the same way since the interest rate is higher.

20

Options to hedge Adverse price movements
(Hedging to opt for a balancing act)

Introduction
An investment position aimed at offsetting potential losses or gains that may be incurred by another investment is a Hedge.

Investments like Hedge helps to reduce losses or gains suffered by an individual or organization, as a result of another investment.

How does it work?

For illustration purposes, let us see how Hedging is used to counter adverse price movements in Currency Risks by what is called the Call Option. We will explain once again everything from what is an Option to What is a Call Option to how it is used to curb an Adverse Price Movement in Currency Risks.

Hedging with Options - Illustration
A Hedge normally is made from financial instruments such as Options, Swaps, Forward Contracts, Exchange Traded Funds, Stocks, etc.

It is used in such a way that it reduces the risk of Adverse Price Movements in an Asset by taking an offsetting position in a related security such as an Option or a Forward Contract.

Before illustrating how options could be used to hedge Adverse Price Movements in Currency Prices, let us take a look at what Options are.

A Currency Option is a contract between a buyer of Currency Options and a Seller of Currency Options. The Buyer of the Option has the right but not the obligation to buy or sell a specified currency at a specified exchange rate before a specified date from the seller of the Option.

However, a seller has an obligation in the event the buyer exercises the right that is bestowed upon him.

Now let us see what are the different types of Options, a Call Option and a Put Option.

A Call Option is where a buyer has the right to buy a specified currency at a specified rate which is the exchange rate at a specified date and a Put Option is where a buyer has the right to sell a specified currency at a specified rate at a specified date to the seller of the option.

The Premium or the Price of the Option is the compensation that the seller of the option receives from the buyer at the time he or she purchases the option.

For illustration purposes, let us assume a trader buys a September Malaysian Rupee 0.10 Call Option for Malaysian Rupee 0.01 Rupee, which means buying a Malaysian Rupee 0.10 Option which guarantees the purchase of 0.10 Malaysian rupee for an Indian Rupee for the buyer of the option.

The premium of the September Malaysian Rupee 0.10 Call Option as it was explained is Malaysian Rupee 0.01.

Now, the trader has the right to buy Malaysian Rupee 0.10 for a Single Indian Rupee using the Malaysian Rupee 0.10 Call Option in the month of September let us say.

Now how it is used to hedge adverse price movement in the Currency Risk for Malaysian Rupee?

Suppose the Malaysian Rupee appreciates above the rate which is the basis of the Malaysian Rupee 0.10 Call Option which is 0.10 to let us say Malaysian Rupee 0.09 or Malaysian Rupee 0.08, that would mean previously for 1 Indian Rupee the trader used to get 0.10 Malaysian Rupee, after the event of Malaysian Rupee appreciation, the trader gets only 0.09 or 0.08 Malaysian Rupee for every Indian Rupee used for the exchange, had he not got the option.

That means, the trader still can get 0.10 Malaysian rupee in September since he has bought the September Malaysian Rupee 0.10 Call Option whereas in comparison, others would only get 0.09 or 0.08 Malaysian rupee for 1 Indian Rupee.

Similarly, the Put Option can be also used by the buyer in the event the Malaysian Rupee depreciates on a similar basis for a Malaysian Rupee 0.10 Put Option.

Hope this clarifies how hedging is used to cover Adverse Price Movements in Currency.

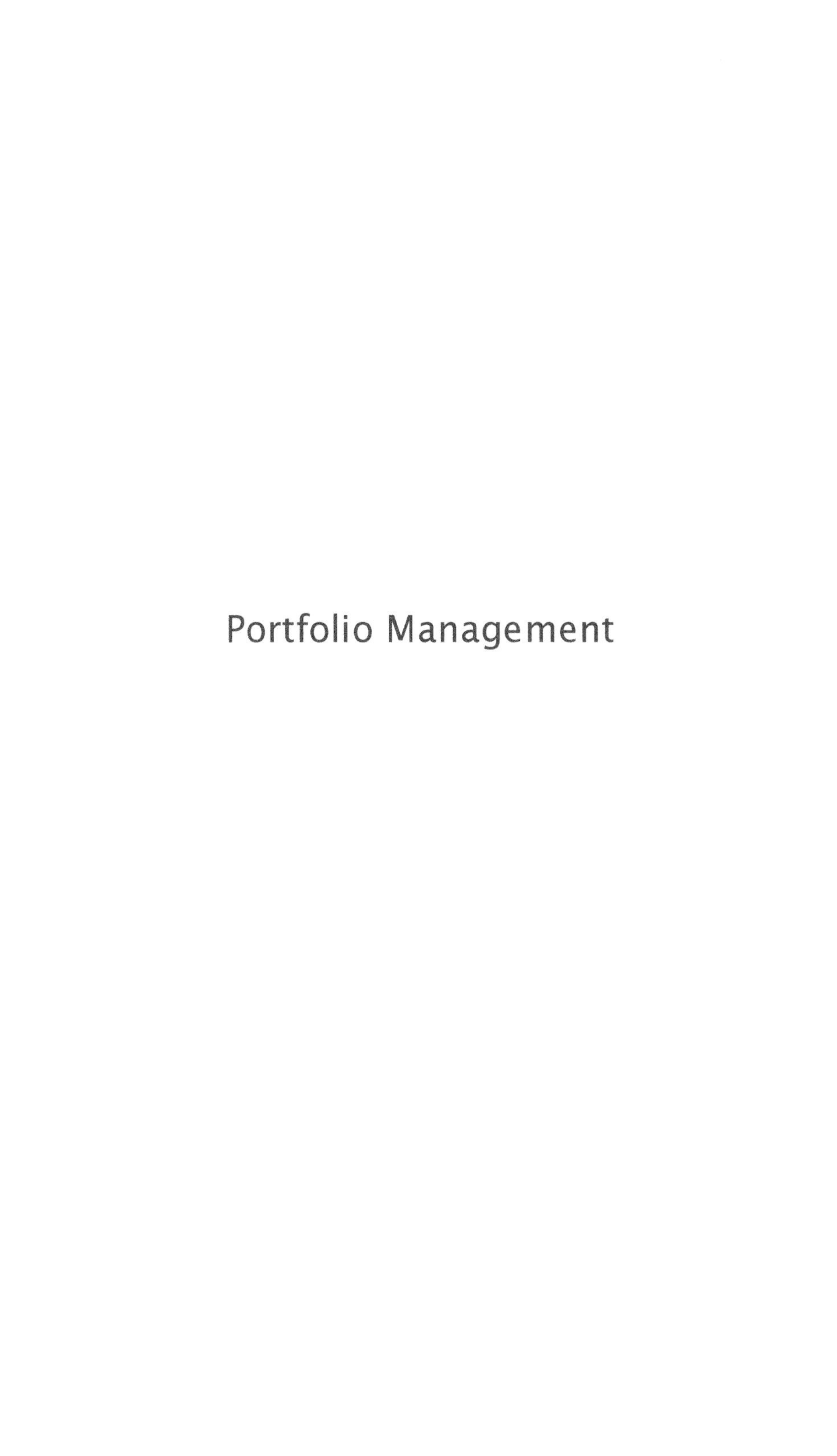

Portfolio Management

21

Wealth Creation

Introduction - Management of Securities

For Wealth Creation through investments in securities, there exist two phases of wealth creation, namely, Security Analysis and Portfolio creation and management.

By way of Security Analysis, what gets selected are securities that have a good potential for growth. Security Analysis also might involve many types of Analysis; Fundamental Analysis: Economy Analysis, Industry Analysis, Company Analysis, Technical Analysis and Market Efficiency Analysis mostly based on the Efficient Market Hypothesis.

After Security Analysis, the securities are bought from the Securities Market which may be Primary Market and Secondary Market or the Stock Exchange. These investments in securities are supposed to fetch returns in the future but since there is an element of uncertainty in any future dealings, there is surely a great amount of risk inherent in any investments in securities.

In other words, any investments in securities invite returns from such investments as well as risks inherent in such investments.

Wealth Creation mandates the investor by properly investing in securities should minimize risks and maximize returns. One of the methods of minimizing risk is diversification of investments, made possible by the creation of a Portfolio for the numerous securities that are bought by the investors.

The Portfolio of investments comprises of different securities and the investor by designing an optimal Portfolio will surely minimize risk and maximize returns.

An alternate risk minimization method is using derivative instruments like Forwards, Futures, Options, and Swaps.

The risks involved in trading assets for investment purposes are also hedged by the use of derivative instruments, which is another way to minimize risks.

For maximizing returns, by evaluating a portfolio, there are two methods, namely the Capital Asset Pricing Model (CAPM) and Arbitrage Pricing Theory which help in the estimation of the expected return of a portfolio which makes sure Portfolio Management is a success-based on any such estimations.

In other words, it is rare to find investors investing their entire savings in a single security. They tend to invest in a group of securities called a Portfolio, which is nothing but a name given to a group of securities that the investor invests their money in.

Portfolio Management – Phases

Portfolio Management is a process that optimizes different activities identified under the different phases such as Security Analysis, Portfolio Analysis, Portfolio Selection, revision, and evaluation.

In this session, we will see what is Security Analysis.

Security Analysis

Buying and selling of securities are part of Investments in securities. Accordingly, the investors can invest in the Primary Market is where the investors directly purchase the securities from the company that is issuing its securities, and from the Secondary market is where the investors purchase and sell securities issued by companies that get traded in the Stock Market (Secondary Market).

Usually, the Stock exchanges provide liquidity to the investments made by the investors in the Corporate and Industrial sectors.

In addition to providing liquidity to the industrial sectors, the stock exchanges also provide Valuation of the stocks that get traded in them.

The National Stock Exchange and Mumbai Stock Exchange are the major National Stock Exchanges in India and in addition, there are several regional stock exchanges in India, the Regulator of these stock exchanges is SEBI, which is also the Regulator for Primary and Secondary Markets.

Various types of securities are available to the investor to invest, to get a faint idea, in India, shares of about 7000 companies are listed in the stock exchanges across the country.

Broadly the securities available in the Industrial or Corporate Sector falls under Ownership and Creditorship.

Securities under Ownership may be Equity Shares and Preference Shares whereas those under Creditorship may be Convertible debentures, Deep Discount Bonds, Zero Coupon Bonds, etc.

In order for the Investor to include securities from the different classifications into a Portfolio of Securities, he has to first do what is called as a Security Analysis.

Hence, Security Analysis is the first step in the Portfolio Management Process. Here the risk return characteristics of each security is thoroughly examined.

In some sense, Security Analysis is where identification of mispriced securities are done, in order to clearly differentiate between under-priced securities and overpriced securities.

In short, this Security Analysis is performed by following two Approaches, namely, Fundamental Analysis and Technical Analysis.

In Fundamental Analysis, an approach to Security Analysis, it concentrates on fundamental factors concerning an enterprise, namely, Earnings Per Share of a company, market share of a company, dividend payout ratio which shows the competition that is faced by the company as well as management or quality of management. A Financial Analyst who follows the Fundamental Analysis, works out the true or intrinsic value of a security based on fundamental factors. If the intrinisic value is lesser than the market price of a share, the share is said to be overpriced and if it is more than the market price of a share, the share is said to be under-priced. Remember, in Fundamental Analysis, the belief is that share price of a company is only determined by the fundamental factors of a company, namely, EPS, Market Share, DPR and Quality of Management.

The benefit of following this method or approach is that the mispricing of shares may lead to an opportunity where the investor can acquire or dispose shares based on whether the shares are under-priced or overpriced, and in doing so, the investor will be staunch in his belief system that the market corrects itself in the future, in order to correctly project the share price of the company.

In short, Fundamental Analysis provides a way for the investor to correctly include shares of strong companies in its portfolio.

The next approach, which is Technical Analysis is where the Analyst believes that there exists a systematic movement in share prices and the share prices in doing so follow a consistent pattern which becomes part of its study. Hence the Technical Analyst, studies the past trends and patterns in share price movements and use it to extrapolate future share prices. Here, a comparison is also made of current share price in the market with the future projected share price and the mispricing is brought to light based on these projections of share prices.

A more recent approach is Efficient Market Hypothesis which believes that the Financial Market is efficient enough to price the shares and all the projected values from Technical Analysis or fundamental factors from Fundamental Analysis according to this school of thought is not required. So, we have covered an overview of Security Analysis and Wealth Creation in this session.

22

Valuation of Shares
(Share Valuation Model)

Intrinsic Value of Share
Each share has what is called the Intrinsic Value of Shares, which are the benefits the holder of the share expects in the future in the form of Capital Appreciation and Dividends. This is also confirmed more by Fundamental Analysis.

According to Fundamental Analysis, if a company's share has in value, intrinsic value lesser than the share's market price, the share is said to be overpriced and sold. If for a share of a company, the intrinsic value of the share is more than the market price, the share is said to be under-priced and bought.

Hence it is important to calculate the intrinsic value of shares and this process is also called as Valuation of Shares.

Typically, to understand the Valuation of shares, it is a must to understand its present value and the Share Valuation Model.

Present Value – A Concept
In Share Valuation process, the present value concept is a fundamental concept and works on the basis of Time Value of Money.

What is Time Value of Money?

Money has a time value and according to this concept, money received today is worth more than money received any time in the future.

This is represented by the equation, F = P ⟦(1+r)⟧ ^n, where F is the future value of money invested today, that is P at interest, r, for n years. Now, this equation is obtained by compounding the present value of money. So, in order to know the present value, the equation should be discounted, accordingly, we obtain, P = F/ ⟦(1+r)⟧ ^n.

Hence, to get Future Value of money, the equation should be a compounding equation and to get Present Value of Money, the equation should be a discounting equation.

So, Present Value of Money is the money that needs to be invested, in order to obtain future value of money.

For example, to get Rs. 500 in 1 year, how much money needs to be invested today, if the rate of interest is 6%. By the equation, it is P=500/ ⟦(1+0.06)⟧ ^1 =500/(1.06)1=479.61.

This would mean, the present value of Rs. 500 after 1 year at interest, 6% is 479.61. Or in other words, Rs. 479.61 needs to be deposited today, in order to get, Rs. 500 after 1 year, at 6% rate of interest.

Share Valuation model – One Year/Multiple Year Holding

Here also, the Present Value Model is used to determine the intrinsic value of a share and that remains to be the

Share Valuation Model. So usually, at the end of the holding period, the major receipts that emerge out of ownership of shares are the sale proceeds of the shares at the end of the holding period, as well as the annual dividends of the shares at the end of the holding period. This can be worked out for One year holding or Multiple Year Holding.

We will illustrate the methods with examples.

One Year Holding Period

The assumption is that, presently someone becomes the shareholder, which means somebody has just bought one share and plans to hold it for 1 year. Correspondingly, he or she can get the benefit out of shares in terms of Dividends received on share till 1 year and the share price amount when he or she disposes of the share at the end of 1 year.

Writing equations, So = D1/ $[(1+k)]$ ^1 +S1/ $[(1+k)]$ ^1 , where So is the present value of share, D1 is the dividend received at the end of 1 year, S1 is the selling price of the share at the end of 1 year.

Multiple Year Holding Period

For multiple year holdings, the shareholder may buy the share now and hold it for a couple or more years and sells it off at the end of the holding period. The present value of the share is represented by the equation, So = D1/ $[(1+k)]$ ^1 + D2/ $[(1+k)]$ ^2 +D3/ $[(1+k)]$ ^3 +…+(Dn+Sn)/ $[(1+k)]$ ^n.

23

Economic Security Analysis

Security Analysis - Introduction

Equity Share, in particular, the intrinsic value of an equity share depends upon the Growth Rate of the company, Earnings of a Company as well as the risk Exposure of a company, which also has a lasting effect on the share price. But we should not forget the fact that the growth rate, earnings, and risk exposure of a company, depend upon the Economic Environment that the company functions in, the industry where the company is part of as well as on the performance of the company itself.

Hence this session concentrates primarily on the Fundamental Security Analysis which we see it to be comprising of

- o Economy Analysis: Wherein we study economy-wide factors such as the Inflation Rate, Growth Rate of the economy, Foreign Exchange Rates, etc
- o Industry Analysis: Where we study factors such as Supply-Demand Gap, Substitute Products, Government Policy changes, etc
- o Company Analysis

Where we study company-specific factors such as Labour Management Relations, Products, and their brand images, the age of the plant as well as quality management.

This session concentrates more on Economic Security Analysis or on the Economic Analysis in Fundamental Security Analysis.

Economy Analysis – Introduction

It can be stated with no doubt that a company performs well when the economy is booming when the incomes rise, demand for products and services increases, and is when the industry and companies tend to prosper. For investors investing in a particular company, they are mostly bothered about some of the economic indicators which affect the performance of a company. A Study on those economic indicators would give the investors an idea about payments of interest and dividends as well as an idea about future corporate earnings for a company.

Hence such a study on Economic indicators is a must and will be complementing a broader study that completes a study on Fundamental Security Analysis.

Economy Study

Growth Rate of National Income:

The economy in general passes through different cycles of prosperity called Economic or Business Cycles, which are Depression, Recovery, Boom, and Recession. Among the four stages, Depression is the worst stage. In this stage of Economic Cycle, the demand for products and services are very low and would be declining. Interest rates and inflation would be seemingly high. Companies will be forced to lay off workers, shut down plants and reduce production which in turn will worsen Manufacturing and Production in the depression cycle.

However, in the next stage of Recovery, there will be signs of economic revival that the different business or industrial segments show. Demand is shown to slowly pick up which in turn will lead to investments in the different walks of the economy. What is seen to rise in this stage are Profits, Employment, and production which will get the economy moving towards the boom phase of the Economic Cycle.

During the Boom phase, a high demand will be shown where the investments and production are maintained at the highest-level catering to a huge demand for products and services. Companies may sore on profits, and after prolonged periods of time, the economy would fall into a recession.

The recession stage is when the economy is slow and there will be a downturn in employment, production, and demand. The profit of companies is shown to decline which will force the economic stage of depression if no appropriate steps are taken by the government.

The growth rate of National Income is characterized by the three main indicators of the National Income of a country, namely, Gross National Product (GNP), Net National Product (NNP), and Gross Domestic Product (GDP). These are different measures of the total income or total economic output of a country, generally. The government of a country makes this data available periodically from time to time.

24

Charting – Basic Principles of Technical Analysis

Technical Analysis – Basic Principles

The following principles are the basic principles in Technical Analysis.

- o   Demand and Supply factors decide the market value of a security operating in a market.
- o   Supply and demand factors of a security are surrounded by rational and irrational factors.
- o   Market movements remain continuous for security prices and behave in such a manner for some time.
- o   Whenever there is a shift in supply and demand factors, the trends in stock prices tend to change.
- o   Charts project patterns and record price movements and these are used by the Analyst making forecasts about price movements.

Charts

Graphical representation of data forms the basis of Technical Analysis and Charting plays an important role or is considered a key activity in Technical Analysis.

Usually, it is the security prices that get charted. For a share that is getting traded in the market, four prices are very important and these are (1) the highest price of the day (2) the lowest price of the day (3) opening price and (4) closing price.

Among the four, again the closing price is the most important because that is what gets used by most Analysts.

To study the share price movements, the price chart is used as the basic tool by Technical Analysts. The prices are plotted on the Y axis and X axis represent the trading days. Here we illustrate three charts, namely, Line Chart, Bar Chart and Japanese Candlestick Chart.

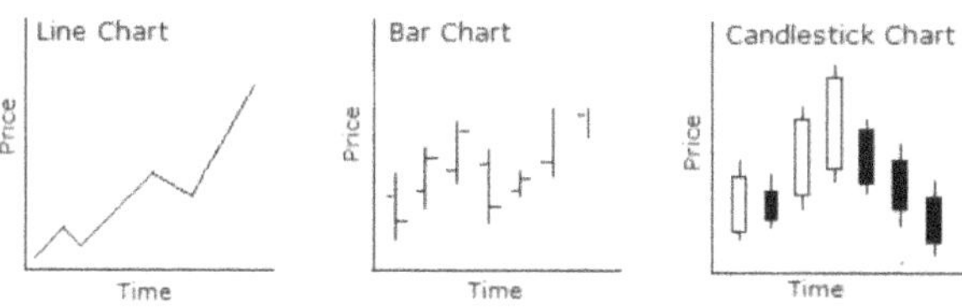

Line Chart

A Line chart may look like this.

The closing price is plotted on Y axis and the trading days are plotted on the X axis.

Bar Chart

It is the most popular chart used in Technical Analysis. In this, the highest price, closing price and the lowest price of a share traded each day is plotted on a day-to-day basis. A Bar Chart is formed by joining the lowest and highest price on a particular day, mostly by a vertical line.

Japanese Candlestick Charts

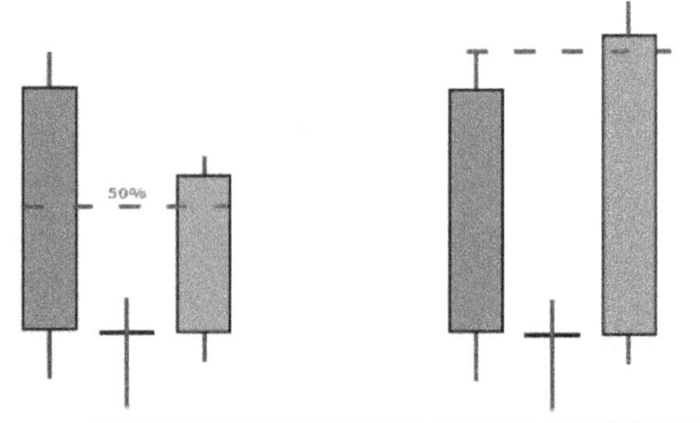

This shows the highest price, lowest price, opening and closing prices of a share on a daily basis. The highest price and the lowest price are joined together by a vertical line. The closing and opening prices of a share is represented by a rectangle that falls between the highest and lowest price of that share on a daily basis. This shape resembles a candlestick and hence the name.

Thus, each daily activity is represented by a candlestick.

Also, there are three types of candlesticks that are usually represented, namely, Doji or neutral, White and Black. A doji represents a share whose closing and opening price of the day are same. A White candlestick represents a bullish trend where closing price of a stock is higher than the opening price on a daily basis.

25

Elliot Wave Theory and Patterns

The behaviour of stock market is predicted by Elliot Wave Theory.

This theory is part of Technical Analysis and is formulated by Ralph Elliot where he has conveyed the formulation of this theory as a result of 75 years of observing the Stock Market movements. He concludes that the stock market movements were very orderly and is seen to follow a pattern of waves.

A wave can be told as a movement of market price with a change in direction from one direction to another. It is the result of buying and selling impulses which are formed from the supply and demand pressures seen in the market. This may result in price reflections which is the direct result of demand and supply pressures on the market.

This theory states that the market moves in waves. Any market movement in a particular direction is represented by five distinct waves. Of the five waves, those in the direction of the movement are termed as impulse waves and those against the movement are termed as corrective waves.

In the figure, waves 1, 3,

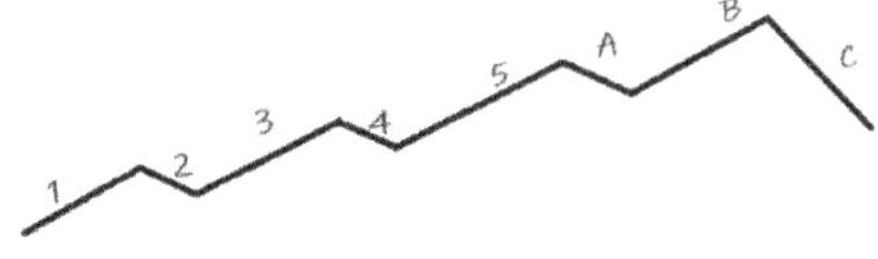

and 5 are impulse waves and waves 2 and 4 are corrective waves. After the five waves, 1,2,3,4 and 5 comes the ABC waves which correct the entire wave pattern from wave 1 to wave 5. Of which, waves A and C are against the trend, and wave B will be along the trend. One complete wave cycle has bearish and bullish waves making up the two distinct phases of market movements.

A fresh cycle of waves follows after the completion of 8 waves movement as suggested by the Elliot Theory.

This theory is used for analysis for prediction of future stock price changes and also decides the investments and when these investments are to be made.

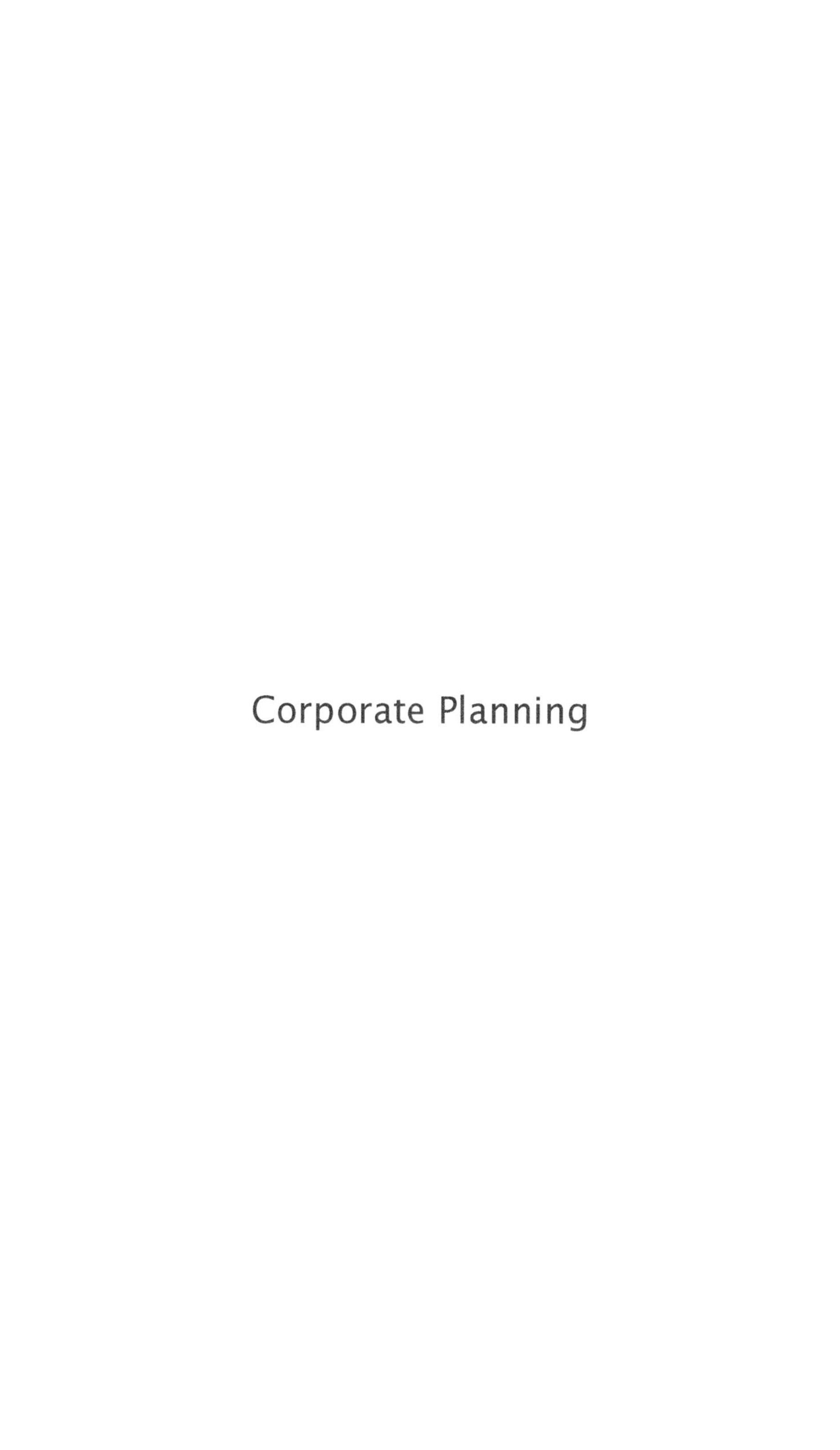

Corporate Planning

26

Capitalization

When long-term obligations of a company are distributed between different classes of owners and creditors, it is called capitalization of an undertaking or capital structure. Capitalization of an undertaking hence depends a lot on Net Income. For investors, the securities and their yields should be comparable to other similar securities, subject to the same risk condition.

Rate of Capitalization

Sometimes prospective earnings of a firm are capitalized, but the rate at which it is capitalized will vary and it depends a whole lot on the subjective measure of risk and would be different for firms in different fields of activities. For a firm, whose income is regular, the rate of capitalization would be lower than the rate of capitalization in the case of a firm that is highly speculative in nature. For new firms, the rate of capitalization is generally way higher than for a firm that is in business for a long time. For the same firm, under different conditions of trade, the rate of capitalization varies depending upon business conditions that are brisk, in which case the capitalization is lower and when the business conditions are slack, the greater risk is involved in capitalization.

Need for Capitalization

Typically, at all phases of the business cycle, the need for capitalization arises, for a firm.

Let us consider the different phases of the business cycle to be the

- o Initial Stage,
- o Growth Stage,
- o Saturation Stage and
- o Existing Period.

In the Initial Stage, the estimation of total funds of capital arises to start the business unit. The main requirements may be Land & Buildings required by the Business Unit as well as Plant & Machinery that needs to be erected in those buildings. Funds may also be required to meet the working capital in the form of Raw Materials, Cash, Components, Stock of Materials, etc.

In the Growth Stage, Finance may be required for Expansion, Introduction of New Technologies, and Programs that are run for the Modernization of the Plant for which Capital needs to be arranged according to a Proper Plan in place.

In the Saturation Stage, most firms may enjoy a high reputation, but Goodwill and Credit Worthiness are required and that can be gained only through Diversification of the Products and it also may help the firm to stay top in the market. For attempts like these, in particular, Product Diversification as well as Improvements of the existing products, huge sums of money are required and it can be arranged through a reorganization of the Capital Structure.

In the Existing Period for any firm, it is so thoughtfully told that Mergers, Acquisitions, and Joint Ventures may happen or may be followed where the economy of the firm may get converted to economies of Mergers between big Giants in the Country. This in most cases is seen to accommodate the Business Establishment and gives them economies of scale of operation. At this stage, the concept of capitalization is very commonly used and has been seen to provide an acceptable formula for the exchange of business terms and capital restructure put to use for efficient and effective practice.

Theories of Capitalization

During the Capitalization of the firm, what gets decided is the number of securities that are offered for Capitalization as well as the appropriate mix that generally has to be designed between debt and equity capital. The final decision of capitalization hence is made after considering the two popular capitalization theories namely, Cost Theory and Earnings Theory.

Let us first see what is Cost Theory.

Cost Theory:

The total value of the Capitalization of an Undertaking is determined based on the total cost of acquiring Fixed Assets and Current Assets of the undertaking. This is arrived at by adding the amount of capitalization that may result in all of, Fixed Assets and Current Assets namely, Cost of Fixed Assets, Amount of Working capital, Cost of Establishment of Business namely Plant & Machinery, Land & Buildings, Cost of Raw Materials, Preliminary Expenses, Flotation Costs of Shares & Debentures, etc.

In other words, Cost Theory helps the promoters to find out the total amount of Capital needed for setting up and establishing of the business. It also implies according to Dockeray that Capitalization at best would be reflective of the value of an enterprise.

The following assumption lies with the Cost Theory,

- o It only considers the Cost of Assets and not the earning capacity of investments,
- o Capitalization made based on Cost does not recognize the fluctuations in earnings that a Company has over a period of time.

Earnings Theory:

According to this theory, capitalization is solely dependent upon the Earning Capacity of the firm. Hence, Profit is in the base of all capitalization. Earnings are also capitalized at the representative rate of return.

Over-Capitalization and Under-Capitalization

A business is said to be over capitalized when,

- o Business has more net assets that it actually requires,
- o Capitalization ends up in excess of the real economic value of assets and,
- o A Fair value is not realized on Capitalization.

For example, whenever there is one of the following conditions namely,

- o The component of equity capital is more in relation to Debt Equity Ratio, given a certain debt or
- o The Long-term funds are not properly deployed on Fixed Assets or
- o If a portion of long-term fund is allocated to Current Assets or

- o The current Assets are not sufficient to meet Current Liabilities, then the condition may result in Over Capitalization.

Normally, Over capitalization is found in companies that deal with depleted assets, namely a mine or an oil rig firm. The condition of Overcapitalization is also known as Water Stock.

In other words, a company is said to be Water Stock, if the shares and debentures of that company far exceeds it true value of fixed assets.

It is also true that the correct indicator of Over Capitalization of a Company is its Earnings. However this condition does not imply an oversupply of funds or a shortage of funds. But it is seen that there are accurate causes for this condition to happen and are mainly, due to,

- o Inflation – Due to inflation, a corporation may acquire assets at a higher price whose book value may fluctuate,
- o Promotional Expense – Promotors may have charged higher promotional expenses,
- o Depreciation – Inadequate depreciation policy
- o Shortage of Capital when funds are very urgently required,
- o Dividend Policy – Some company may adopt a lenient dividend policy in order to appease the shareholder which may result in Over Capitalization.

Effects of Over-capitalization

Over-capitalization has gruelling effects on Corporations, Consumers, Society and Owners.

For Corporations, this may mean difficulty in raising new funds or capital. Some of the workarounds like artificial devices in reducing depreciation or maintenance charges are seen to further aggravate the Water Stock conditions.

For Consumers, the prices of the products that are offered by the company may go up.

For Owners, they are the biggest losers. Because of a fall in the market value of shares, they may be at a huge disadvantage and may have lost a chance to dispose off their holdings. Society may render itself to tough competition and may witness the gradual closing down or liquidation of firms.

It is also seen that conditions of Excessive Debts and Over Capitalization exists in many firms.

Hence in order to correct Over Capitalization, the following methods are seen to benefit the company that is facing Over Capitalization namely,

- o Reduction in Interest Rates on Bonds (Only possible if Company goes for Reorganization. Also, the refunding operation may sometimes get enough in interest payment savings of Bonds).
- o Reduction in Funded Debt (Only possible if the Company goes for Reorganization)
- o Redemption of Preferred Stock if it carries a higher dividend (since funds for redemption comes from sale of Common Stock but if there are arrears in Preference Stock, this may not be the right approach)

- o Reduction in par value of stock (Sometimes it is an impossible task because of stockholder's belief of the importance of par-value)
- o Reducing shares of Common Stock (provided the Shareholders agree).

Under-Capitalization

Under-capitalization is not a condition resulting from a lack of funds, it actually refers to the amount of outstanding stock. It is infact the reverse of Over-capitalization.

It comes as a result of,

- o Underestimating of future earnings at the time of promotion,
- o Increase in earnings from later events or activities,
- o When company earns sufficient income to meet its fixed interest, fixed dividend charges, and is able to offer a better rate on its equity shares.

Causes of Under-Capitalization

Some of the more common causes of Under-Capitalization is Underestimation of Earnings (actual earnings may be higher that the value is not properly reflected), Underestimation of funds, because of conservative dividend policy, retained earnings may have resulted in a huge amount of savings, a shift from an adverse business climate to a prosperous one may result in under-capitalization.

Remedies of Under-Capitalization

The two main methods by which under-capitalization can be prevented are by,

- o Stock Dividend: If there is enough surplus, the corporation can declare a dividend payable in stock which increases the market value because of effective capitalization.
- o Stock split up: where by the corporation offers several shares of new stock for every share of old stock. This reduces the par-value with an increase in number of shares, given the capital stock account is never affected. This will decrease the Earnings per share because of increase in number of shares and because of rate of earnings remaining constant (increase in shares, reduction in par value per share). This results in condition of Capitalization with minimal changes and EPS reduced.

Corporate Restructuring

27

Corporate Restructuring

In the growing phase of a Company, it is extremely difficult for a firm to stay away from Corporate Restructuring without which, the firm may not survive in the long run. Usually, for identifying business opportunities and threats, Scanning of Environment is extremely helpful. It is also important to acknowledge the fact that corporate restructuring is necessary whenever the business environment changes.

This will most often be marked by increased competition and subtle changes that affect Liberalization, Globalization, and Privatization.

If a firm reaches a consensus, that Globalization is the way forward or offers a lot of opportunities for the firm, the firm has to restructure as a means of competing with new entrants, or by the manufacture of new products and services at high-quality and at a reasonable price.

The restructuring of a company also involves experimenting with new tools and ideas. Many firms try to turn around a business by buying other companies, selling off the unprofitable business, splitting the company as well as cutting jobs in the concern.

In most cases, the company would be able to maximize profits by externally merging with other firms or by acquiring another firm. The strategy of the company hence is simple, maximizing profits in the form of Mergers, Acquisitions, Amalgamation, Takeover, absorption, consolidation, etc.

We will briefly go through each of these aspects while we cover Corporate Restructuring from the viewpoint of Management activity!

Meaning

What is Corporate Restructuring?

Corporate Restructuring is a management term for the act of partially dismantling and reorganizing a company so that it remains profitable and efficient in the long run. It involves selling off a portion of the company or making severe reductions in the workforce by way of staff reductions. Restructuring is always done as part of a Bankruptcy of a firm or of a takeover attempt of the company in question by another firm. It may also be done as an initiative from a new CEO of a company when he or she tries to make difficult and controversial decisions in an attempt to save or reposition the company in question.

Translating into a series of activities, Corporate Restructuring expands or contracts a firm's operations and modifies its financial structure and brings about significant change in its organizational structure and in its internal functioning.

Taking under its fold, activities such as mergers, buyouts, take over, business alliances, etc it always completes all performance improvement initiatives and results in organizational restructuring by maximizing profits.

The following reasons exist for Corporate Restructuring, namely,

- o Higher Earnings (restructuring is attempted by selling off loss-making units and retaining higher earnings),
- o Ensuring clarity in vision, strategy, and structure,
- o Provides proactive leadership,
- o Empowerment of employee,
- o Leveraging of Core Competency
- o Re-engineering attempts, and
- o Making constant business alliances.

Forms of Corporate Restructuring

The following forms of Corporate Restructuring exist and are real. Privatization forms an important part of Corporate Restructuring. Some of the different forms of Corporate Restructuring are,

- o Expansion,
- o Mergers,
- o Amalgamation,
- o Take-over, and
- o Joint Venture.

Expansion

This form increases the capacity of an organization and does not normally involve spending on any technical expertise or abilities. In the Expansion of business, more funds are raised in the form of Debt or Equity and the funds so raised are used to finance Fixed Assets required for the manufacturing of Expanded Levels of Production. A Cloth Manufacturer increases its machine layout in order to accommodate increased production of Linen may be Expansion.

Merger

Combination of two or more companies into a single company where one survives and others perish and lose their corporeal existence is Merger. The acquired company or survivor acquires assets as well as liabilities of the Merged Companies. Hence if the buyer A Inc buys B Inc and C Inc, the survivor is mostly A Inc which retains its identity and the seller in other words is extinguished and goes out of business.

All Assets, Liabilities, and stock of one company stands transferred to Transferor company in consideration of payment in the form of Transferee Company's equity shares or debentures or cash or a mix of the two.

Mergers may be Horizontal Merger or Vertical Merger or Conglomerate Merger.

A Horizontal-mergers takes place between companies operating in the same industry. Vertical Merger on the other hand is where two or more companies making spare parts of a product, merges under one product offering. Conglomerate mergers are between two companies who have nothing in common which is also called pure conglomerate merger and if it has no overlapping interest but serves to further product extensions, then it gets called as mixed conglomerate merger.

Amalgamation

Amalgamation is like merger only difference is that a new company takes over two or more existing companies. For example, if a new Company XYZ Inc takes over A Inc, B Inc and C Inc, it is called Amalgamation.

Take Over

Take-over is acquisition where the major differences are in the Approach followed to Business Combinations, also the process of takeover, transactions, determination of share exchange or cash price and goals fulfilment are all different. For example, in Takeover, the process is unilateral, offeror company decides the maximum price etc.

Joint Venture

A Joint Venture is the setting up of an independent legal entity, in which two or more separate firms participate. The Joint Venture agreement clearly indicates how the cooperating members will share ownership, operational responsibilities and financial risks and rewards. For example, no single oil exploration company has resources to build a pipeline to transport oil across continents.

Hence, Joint Venture were made ensuring participation of many different oil companies.

So, this completes a basic understanding of Corporate Restructuring.